DISCOVER
IN THE GAME OF LIFE
YOUR PHOENIX

Activate Authenticity and
Follow Life Missions

HIROYUKI "HIRO" MIYAZAKI

First Edition

Author website: https://www.PhoenixBlessing.com.

Discover Your Phoenix in the Game of Life/Hiroyuki "Hiro" Miyazaki.-

ISBN 978-1-09832-451-3 (Printed Book);
ISBN 978-1-09832-452-0 (eBook)

Ordering information: https://store.bookbaby.com.

Front cover image © chesterf /Stockfresh; all other images Hiroyuki Miyazaki

First Edition

CONTENTS

The phoenix is flying across time and space,
arriving at the crossroads of your life.

Doubt, and she'll disappear into thin air.

Chase, and she'll slip through your fingers like desert sand.

Surrender, and she'll show you the way to your destiny.

Hiroyuki "Hiro" Miyazaki

PREFACE

Who am I? What's the purpose of life? Where do I go after death?

I am a healer, coach, and teacher of meditation and emotional healing. I used to work at a corporate job but switched careers in 2008. When I started meditating, I hoped to find answers to life's biggest questions; however, it wasn't that easy. In every meditation session, I was far from being in a meditative state because my mind was full of distracting thoughts about my work, life situations, the future, and regret from past experiences. My meditation teacher told me to continue every day regardless. And he was right. As time passed, I learned to calm those thoughts and emotions, and gradually, I became able to reach a calm and peaceful state during my meditations.

With time, I also started to notice a feeling arising inside of my heart during my meditations. It was a nice, warm, and comforting feeling, as if somebody was telling me "Hiro, everything is going to be fine." Every time I meditated, I looked for the feeling and enjoyed getting a taste of it. Eventually, I noticed there were more feelings inside my heart, and each of them seemed to have different messages. If I tried to grab them, they disappeared. But if I just relaxed and allowed them to slowly arise, I was able to experience them. Each of them gave me nice feelings, but they were all different and seemed to have different messages attached to them. I did my best to interpret their meanings.

"All you need is within."

"You are loved by everyone and everything around you."

"You are worthy and eternal."

This is how I started receiving intuitive messages from inside my heart. Every day, during my meditation, I received intuitive messages and took note of them. The messages were sort of generic and broad in meaning, and it was sometimes hard to understand whether they had practical use in real life, but I kept taking notes.

As I began to dive deeper into my spiritual practice, I started teaching meditation and hosting private healing sessions. In my private sessions, I avoided quick fixes that solved surface-level problems, and instead, went deeper into my clients' situation and identified certain lessons they could learn from it. Yes, lessons, not the cause. Every problem or challenge in life has an underlying lesson that needs to be learned by the client. When the lesson is learned, they can heal their heart, and the situation resolves by itself. Then, the purpose of challenge is fulfilled. Through private healing sessions, I have touched people in their hearts, and helped them identify their lessons and overcome their challenges. I've also received intuitive messages, such as:

"Liberate yourself by forgiving others."

"Remember who you truly are."

"This is the divine timing you planned for your life."

Each of these messages had a profound healing effect on the client and provided important insights into my initial questions. I took note of those, too.

After over ten years of meditation and thousands of private sessions, I was finally able to connect the dots of those bits and pieces of intuitive insights, and portray a bigger picture of what's really happening in our lives, which answered all my questions. It's a long answer that describes a system of life, which I call the Game of Life Theory. It gives us a different perspective on why challenges happen in our lives, how we can solve them for good, and how we can create the biggest joy and fulfillment in life.

One of the most important things I learned through those intuitive insights was that there is no enemy in our lives but fear. Fear is the enemy that causes misfortunes and unhappiness. Fear is what stops us from connecting to our hearts. If you don't know what you want in your heart, how can you be truly happy? Instead of fighting against each other, we humans can join forces in conquering our fears.

The information in this book will enable you to conquer your fears, rediscover who you truly are, and create joy and fulfillment in your life. And I believe many people in the world need to receive what I've put together in this book.

So here I am. This is my theory about life.

With love and gratitude,
Hiroyuki "Hiro" Miyazaki

PROLOGUE

Numerous souls are gathered in an open field that's filled with bright lights. There is no sound or wind but a prevailing energy of peace and warmth. Every soul is radiating a beautiful light in different colors—white, dark blue, green, violet, yellow, gold, and many more.

Just like everyone else, you are ready to go into the Game of Life, waiting for the perfect time to make the jump. Ever since you decided to join the game, you've done a lot of preparation to fulfill your wishes. You've promised a group of other souls you'd go with them, you've chosen a birth location and a birthdate, and you've chosen a birth mother and a physical body. You've also arranged some important events and meetings, made promises with other souls to help each other along the way, and agreed to play certain roles to create effective learning situations for all souls involved. You are looking forward to entering this life very much!

In addition to making major progress in your spiritual growth, you will meet many of your soul family members in different roles—some as family members or romantic partners, and others as mentors, students, friends, colleagues, competitors, enemies, or strangers. With them, you'll be able to experience various thoughts, emotions, and physical sensations you've never had before.

You are aware that once you go into a human life, you will lose access to the same awareness and memory you have now. You're hoping to discover your Phoenix, but you never know how life will evolve with its free will. Still, you are excited, even about the uncertain parts of the game, because it makes the experience more enriching and deep. Even if things deviate from your original plan, you can go with the flow, make the necessary adjustments, and fulfill your purposes in this lifetime.

"Bye, everyone! See you later!"

Many other soul family members have already departed into this lifetime. Finally, it is coming close to your divine timing. You look at your birth mother as she patiently waits for you on Planet Earth. She's ready. You take a deep breath, jump into the iridescent gate, and travel down a long tunnel of light into a tiny physical body you'll spend this Game of Life living in.

Game on!

INTRODUCTION

Have you discovered the Phoenix in your life? Do you know the meaning of your challenges and where they are guiding you?

Happiness starts with knowing what you really want, the intrinsic desires that are coming from your soul. The purpose of *Discover Your Phoenix in the Game of Life* is to help you experience happiness, joy, and fulfillment in your heart. In the process, you will discover your Phoenix, your life-changing transformations and a renewed sense of identity that will successfully guide you through life.

My grandfather was a soldier who survived the war, and my grandmother's family ran Terakoya, a humble temple-run school, during wartime. Her ancestors included a brave Samurai warrior, who fought against political leaders for the freedom of the people. My grandmother once showed me a Samurai sword that was used by our ancestors—a long, shining metal that had a sharp edge on one side. It was scary yet beautiful at the same time. One day, she said to me, "You don't need this anymore, Hiro. Today, you use your brain to make your way."

That was the family my father was born into. As the first boy in the family, people had a lot of high expectations for him; they wanted him to become a great man, succeed in society, and take good care of the entire family. This was the post-war era, and people had dropped their swords and firearms long before, so the definition of a "great man" was maintaining the highest integrity, being the smartest guy everywhere he went, winning every competition, and being successful in society as a businessman. If he were to live up to their expectations, people would be proud of him, and say, "You are a good boy." But if he didn't, he would have been deemed a failure. Because of this environment, the purpose of my father's life—at least in the beginning—was to be the "good boy"—the successful businessman.

And he did well. He studied hard and made good marks in every evaluation he went through; his academic record was outstanding. When my father was well into his career, he realized that his boss, the CEO of the company, was making a terrible decision. Driven by one of his core values—maintaining the highest integrity—my father gathered up his courage and confronted his boss, risking his job in the process.

"Boss, this is too risky. This could potentially push all our employees out of the company to live on the street," he said.

The boss didn't take his criticism well, and my father was fired from the company. This put him off course from the "successful" life as defined by his elders, which was unfortunate, but it lifted a weight off his shoulders. He was finally liberated from the expectations of others and could take a moment to pause, look at his life from a different perspective, and ask himself: *What do I really want in life?*

Some months later, my mother gathered our family members at the dinner table. She seemed serious and determined, and I sensed something important was taking place. With everyone present, she said: "Today, I want you all to know that your father has decided to follow a new life path. Let's celebrate your father's new journey and give him all our support."

She told us he would be pursuing his artistic passions, such as stained glass arts. I remember looking at his face in that moment, and the stressed, nervous, suppressed look I had come to know was completely gone. His face shone like the sun—joyful, playful, and happy. It was the most beautiful expression I had ever seen him make. I didn't understand what he was about to start, but I was convinced it was what he was born to do.

Your Phoenix

Your Phoenix is your authentic higher self that knows why you were born into this lifetime, what you really want, and where you are heading. As the process of discovering your authenticity involves letting go of the old and rebirthing into a new life, "Phoenix" works very well as a metaphor to convey the transformational process and the magnitude of its importance for one's life. Your Phoenix, or your authentic identity, contains your most deeply held beliefs, your values, and the principles you live by. When your Phoenix reveals itself, it fuels you with a deep sense of purpose that burns brightly with the fire of your passion.

Everyone is born with this innate identity as Phoenix, but many of us lose contact with it during our adolescent years, distracting ourselves from following our hearts. In the process, our brains take the driver's seat in our lives, while our Phoenix becomes hidden and dormant. As a result, many of us experience a lack of joy, fulfillment, and purpose in life.

However, your Phoenix does not stay quiet forever. From time to time, it attempts to talk to you through your heart, usually when your thoughts or actions go against your authentic identity and cause conflicts inside yourself. If you ignore this inner voice, it grows bigger and louder, and it never stops until you face it head-on. Often, this causes major life challenges that trigger deep-seated fears and emotional turmoil. It drags you down and makes your life miserable. You can try to address the situation on the surface, but the same challenge will keep coming back over and over again. You might turn your back and give up on your dreams, yourself, or your life, but this is exactly the moment when you can discover your Phoenix and make your life shine.

A challenging situation can turn into an opportunity that offers precious gifts and lessons that trigger breakthroughs, revelations, realizations, or whatever major transformations are needed in your life. The harder the challenge, the bigger the transformation. Your Phoenix reveals itself when you release the old and open yourself to the new, whether it be an idea, belief, lifestyle, behavioral pattern, career, or relationship. Just like the legendary bird that burned the old into ashes and rose from it into a new identity, the Phoenix within you arrives in your life, pushes out the old that no longer serves you, and invites your authenticity to flourish.

Game of Life

When you think of challenges as opportunities to discover your authentic identity and fulfill your purpose and missions in life, you meet life as a game to be played. Suppose you are a soul who signed up to this Game of Life and assumed a human body. You carefully arranged events and opportunities beforehand so you can grow step by step until you reach a point where you make a major breakthrough and reveal your Phoenix identity, thereby fulfilling your purpose and missions and becoming who you are meant to be. I bet this sounds like an audacious theory, but it explains a lot of life's mysteries, shows you a way to let go of your fears, and can empower you to flourish. So I ask you to be open-minded and stay with me to view your life as if you're starring in a heroic story that includes both comedy and tragedy, and progresses toward finding treasures that feed your soul.

Discover Your Phoenix

Discovering your Phoenix is not easy. You need to conquer your fears and take risks to change your life. It may take you many years to find it, as was the case for me. This book does not contain easy steps or simple formulas to discover your Phoenix; it takes the opposite approach.

Discovering your Phoenix requires you to review your major life challenges, retrieve lessons, and activate your authenticity. It takes contemplation, focus, courage, compassion, and acceptance. Ultimately, you must take responsibility for your development. You must devote yourself to personal development to realize your potential.

- Part I examines the theory of the Game of Life as a guideline on how to view your life to support your journey toward authenticity.

- Part II offers insights into important challenges that may show up in your life, and gives guidance on how to turn them into opportunities to discover your authentic identity and fulfill your purpose and missions in life.

In each chapter, you will find a series of exercises to facilitate healing and invite important realizations to arise. If you are interested in continuing your journey further, I offer private sessions, guided visualizations, and workshops to help your growth and alignment to your life missions. Visit my website at https://www.phoenixblessing.com for details.

By dedicating yourself to discovering your Phoenix, you will become an authentic presence who can make a positive difference in the world and leave a legacy for others to follow.

Part I:
GAME OF LIFE THEORY

ACCIDENTAL OR PREPLANNED?

In January 2007, I flew to Egypt with ten friends. We did the typical sight-seeing, like visiting various pyramids, shopping at the bazaar, going to the museum, and so on. But we did one thing that was not typical: We stayed a little longer in the Great Pyramid and meditated in the King's Chamber. The chamber was dimly lit and humid. Other tourists came in and out, taking pictures and talking about the sarcophagus in various languages, but we sat down on the floor and meditated for some time. I didn't have extraordinary vision during that meditation session, but I felt myself go deeper within than I ever had before. When I opened my eyes, I felt so refreshed and confident, and I stood tall. I had this feeling that something new was about to start.

Immediately after I returned to Japan from Egypt, one of my friends introduced me to a meditative healing technique. She said, "You can change your subconscious beliefs in seconds!" I had doubts, but I was also curious. I thought it might help me overcome some behavioral patterns that were hindering my work performance. Back then, I was stressed at work, and was looking for ways to control my emotions better and experience more peace of mind.

The healing technique turned out to be a very good one. I felt a change within, was able to manage my emotions better, and was less stressed than I used to be. As I continued to study the healing technique and practice it with my friends and colleagues, I found myself experiencing a sweet, warm feeling in my heart every time I did the healing on myself and others. I didn't know how or why I was feeling that way, but it was clear that my heart was happy. Gradually, I yearned to experience that feeling as much as I could for the rest of my life. After months of inner struggles, I finally made an important decision to change my career from a corporate job to healing and coaching. That decision changed the course of my life completely. (I will discuss the inner struggles leading up to it later.)

In the years since making that decision, I have traveled to other countries to offer my healing consultations and have helped thousands of people overcome their challenges and create positive changes in their lives. My clients have been in all types of situations, like business downturns, miserable relationships, health challenges, finance challenges, and so on. One day, a woman came to me with a newborn baby, and said, "Hiro, thank you for helping me break up with my ex-boyfriend last year. Since then, I was able to find the love of my life, and now I have this beautiful boy."

This conversation got me thinking; if I didn't make the unconventional career move from a corporate employee to a healer, this baby might not exist today. The career move was such an unlikely one for me, and there was more than 90% chance of me not taking that path. It seemed so accidental. And yet, the innocent smile of that baby didn't seem like an accident at all; that beautiful, radiant smile on his face and the effect it was having on others was so profound, eternal, and divine. In my heart, I knew that baby was meant to be born, and we were meant to meet at that moment and be inspired by his presence, as with all others who were present at that moment.

I wouldn't have been able to meet that baby without a unique chain of events—my friend's introduction to healing, meeting the founder, traveling to other countries, meeting this woman for healing, and so on. It's easy to say that all those events were accidental or coincidental, but what if they all were meant to happen so we could arrive at the right place at the right time?

In life, there are some important events or important meetings that make profound impacts on the course of our lives. For Helen Keller, the meeting with Anne Sullivan changed her life completely. Paul McCartney met John Lennon and formed the most successful songwriting partnership in history. With his partnership with Steve Jobs, Steve Wozniak invented the Apple I computer. For Anthony Robbins, his adversity of living on his own at the age of seventeen led him to Jim Rohn, who gave him a chance to learn, grow, and make an impact on others' lives. These people made (and are still making) profound impacts on the lives of others, and they each had some chance encounters that seem to have happened accidentally on the surface, but were so essential for their contributions to the world. The big question is: were they just lucky to have those events and meetings that guided them to their life path? Or, were all those events predestined to happen?

Let's say all life events and meetings happen either accidentally or coincidentally.

On one day, you might experience happiness, but the next day, you might experience misfortune that makes you suffer. Life is volatile, uncertain, complex, and ambiguous. This perspective activates various fears—fear of survival, fear of losing your quality of life, fear of losing love, fear of being alone, fear of having no meaning in life, and so on. In the quest for security and certainty, you are pushed to compete with others to fight over money, fame, and power. Eventually, this becomes the purpose of your life, and your vision and values reflect the same. But no matter how much you win, the fears do not go away; instead, they aggravate. You end up even more afraid of losing what you have, and you still don't have peace of mind. And you say, "What's the meaning of it all?"

Alternatively, let's say some life events and meetings are preplanned to happen for the benefit of your life purpose. You experience events and meetings that guide you to become who you are meant to be and do what you are meant to do. You trust that everything in life happens for a reason. You may sometimes experience misfortune, but you can still maintain peace of mind because you know even misfortune teaches you a necessary lesson to get one step closer to who you are meant to be. With this perspective, you feel safe and supported, have faith in your life, and can live in peace and with gratitude for everything that happens.

We all have a choice to believe that life events are either coincidental or preplanned.

What will you choose?

It is essentially a choice between fear and faith. These two options offer totally different perspectives of life that will impact your experiences and outcomes. When I posed this choice to myself years ago, I realized this question caused an inner conflict between my brain and my heart. My brain said that life events are all accidental, while my heart said otherwise. I spent many years trying to figure this out, and now I have a theory that my brain and heart finally agree on.

The Game of Life Theory explains that you were born into this life for a purpose, and before this life, you preplanned important events and meetings so you could grow and fulfill that purpose. You entered this life without conscious awareness of such blueprints and depend on your free will to go about your life's path. Does this theory portray the truth about our lives? I invite you to answer this question only after reading this book.

Regardless, this theory explains a lot about the many mysteries of our lives and can be very useful in conquering our fears and effectively addressing various life situations, thereby enabling us to create the utmost joy and fulfillment in life.

1. GAME OVERVIEW

Human life is a role-playing game. Players assume the roles of characters and take responsibility for acting out those roles within a lifetime through literal acting and effective decision-making in the realm of character development.

- The object of the Game of Life is to live a life in a human body and satisfy all desires (body, mind, and spirit) as much as possible through various life events on Planet Earth.

- When you step into the body, it becomes "awake," and you live a life as your body. You need to step out of the body regularly and enter a "sleeping" state for routine maintenance.

- Your body lives in a physical environment; therefore, your activity as the body is influenced by the laws of the physical universe, as well as physical qualities, relationships, communities, and nature.

- The Game of Life is like playing a heroic story that includes both comedy and tragedy, and makes you progress toward finding treasures that feed your soul.

- You can prearrange for some events and meetings to take place during your human life to help you fulfill your purpose; however, once you are in your body, you are on your own. You have free will to do whatever you want, even if it's against the preplanned events and meetings you set for yourself. If that's the case, you will need to adjust your plan accordingly.

- Over the course of a lifetime, you will have plenty of opportunities to enjoy a physical experience in a human body, attain spiritual growth, and contribute to others' spiritual growth.

Here are some important implications. First, you entered this game—a human life—by your own free will. You were not forced, and you didn't have to play, but you really wanted to take this opportunity. The purpose of life is for your soul to grow, and you have the freedom to set the level of growth you need to attain in this lifetime and plan accordingly. Second, all your life experiences are illusions generated by the physical laws of the universe. These illusions are effective in providing you with an environment for your growth, but your true essence resides beyond the physical realm. Third, no life is above or below others, regardless of their experiences in human life. Every experience gives you knowledge and aids in your growth; therefore, every life is special, precious, and valuable. Human judgment of right/wrong, rich/poor, and success/failure is not relevant to the worthiness of a person from the perspectives of our souls.

With this, let's go over the key concepts of the Game of Life Theory.

Player of the Game

Have you ever played a video game? You assume the role of a character to play the game, whether it is a warrior, athlete, car, or animal. These characters are a vehicle for you to play the game, but the vehicles are not the players—you are.

The game of human life works the same way. Human bodies are not the players, they are just vehicles. Well, then, who are the players? This is possibly one of the most inevitable yet deep questions. It's like, "who am I really?"

To answer this question, let's use the example of a human called Michael. If you ask him who he is, he would say, "I am Michael." For everyone, including himself, his physical body is the expression of his identity. In this perspective, the following equation applies:

$$I = Michael = This\ physical\ body$$

In the Game of Life, the physical body is just a vehicle of the game; therefore, this consciousness that says "I" is not equal to the physical body. Instead, the consciousness *has* the body, and the body is named 'Michael.' With this, the following statement portrays the relationship more accurately:

I have this physical body named Michael.

Now, if you ask who this is without a body and a name, the only way to describe this consciousness is:

I am.

This is it. "I am" is the player—a consciousness that exists, thinks, and feels. It does not need a physical body, but it has a physical body in the Game of Life. If it wants to, it can join multiple games of life at the same time and enjoy all the experiences each game offers. Some people might call "I am" different names—soul, higher self, subconscious, or super conscious, to name a few. I prefer to call it a "soul" hereon.

You are not your body. You are a soul that has a body. Someday, your physical body will cease to exist, but you will continue to exist as a consciousness, and that is eternal.

Purpose, Goals, Missions

For a car racing video game, perhaps the purpose of the game is to have fun and excitement. The mission would be each car race, and the goal would be to win all the races in the shortest amount of time.

Now, let's examine the purpose, goals, and missions for the Game of Life. As a soul that exists beyond physical reality, you do not need physical objects, such as money, a car, a house, physical health, or physical beauty. The purpose is something more meaningful, beyond the physical realm. If you close your eyes for a moment, you can experience the state beyond the physical realm. That's right; it's that black space where you think, imagine, and feel. This is the space where your consciousness lives, and it does not disappear, even after your physical death. Whatever you gain through the Game of Life must be meaningful in this world beyond the physical. So, what might that be?

It is the state of mind. Through a human life, you (your soul) wanted to improve your state of mind. In your mind, you can experience various states. You can have low-vibrational states, such as fear, sadness, and anger, or you can have high-vibrational states, like love, joy, and fulfillment. Through a human life, you experience various situations that put you in a low-vibrational state, giving you the opportunity to activate virtuous qualities to maintain a high-vibrational state or go even higher. Growing spiritually through activating more virtuous qualities is the purpose of the Game of Life.

As a soul, you already have all the virtuous qualities within you, but you need to activate them to reflect them in your state of being. A virtuous quality can be activated when there is an opportunity to use it. As souls, we wanted to join this Game of Life so we could create various situations to activate virtuous qualities, such as kindness, patience, tolerance, compassion, honesty, integrity, and so on. For example, how can you activate tolerance? You need a situation that requires tolerance. If tolerance is one of the virtues you want to develop, you as a soul would have arranged such situations to take place in your life. Note that each virtuous quality has different levels of mastery. There are infinite shades of gray between the lowest level of kindness and the highest level; therefore, to activate as many virtuous qualities as possible, your soul would elect to play this Game of Life again and again.

Before every Game of Life, you set spiritual growth goals to attain throughout your lifetime. Growth goals depend on how much you've already attained throughout your past lives and how much and in what areas you want to attain in this lifetime. For example, you might choose to attain a higher level of compassion, address your short temper, and cultivate mindfulness in this lifetime.

In addition to growth goals, you also planned some missions in life to contribute to others' growth. Missions are promises between souls to support each other's spiritual growth. Missions can be as profound as inspiring millions of people, or it could be as humbling as helping your family and friends. You can share your experience, give advice, and inspire them to grow. It does not matter how many souls you help. It matters how you feel and grow through being of service to others. Goals and missions are the real reasons behind difficult challenges and events in life, and it is possible to figure them out by reviewing what you've experienced in your life so far. Recognizing your goals and missions will give you clarity on what you want in life and where you are heading.

Another important purpose of the Game of Life is to enjoy a physical reality. As a soul, living a human life is a precious and fascinating opportunity to experience a physical body, nature, and relationships with other souls, and witness various levels of qualities in yourself and others.

Life Planning

You decided to come into this lifetime for your growth, missions, and physical experiences. To create a good chance of fulfilling them, you carefully planned your life and chose your persona, environment, family members, body, birthdate and birth time, community, events, and meetings.

Family

Family members largely influence your physical, mental, emotional, and spiritual construct during adolescence, and thus, make a huge impact on the quality of your entire life. They can allow your virtuous qualities to flourish, so you can start your mission early in life, or they can cause pains from which you can grow. They greatly influence the trajectory of your life path. Through your parents and family members, you learn how to love and be loved, your worthiness, what a man-woman relationship should be, what the purpose of life might be, and possible visions for the future. They also help you establish habits and disciplines, and give you lots of beliefs about everything in life. All of these affect your adulthood.

Because of their strong influence, you choose your family members and/or guardians carefully, and make promises with them to aid in each other's growth. But that's not the only reason. You have some souls that are dear to you, and you can choose to be born with them in a family and spend quality time together. It is not surprising that a group of souls that choose to be born together across lifetimes is called a 'soul family.'

Of course, the choice of family environment is not limited to birth parents; sometimes souls choose to be adopted by other parents. Other times, souls choose not to have dedicated parent figures and spend adolescence in an orphanage instead. All these different environments give souls precious themes and opportunities for their development that later flourish as gifts and talents in their lives.

Soul family members might be your parents in one life, sisters/brothers in the next life, or a spouse or friends in another life. You might also choose to encounter them as a boyfriend or girlfriend, husband or wife, a parent or a child, or relatives. When a soul decides to be born as the child of a dear soul, and pregnancy does not work as expected, the baby's soul waits for another chance and keeps trying. If that doesn't work, the baby might choose to come as a grandchild, an adopted child, in-laws, or even a colleague at a workplace. Spending quality time with dear ones, even if it's a short period of time, enriches our heart and soul. Once determined, our souls manage to make it happen, no matter what it takes. In relationships with a dear soul, you'll feel comfortable with them from the first day, even if you've never seen the person before; it will be easy to experience joy, warmth, and a deeper connection with them.

Body

When you entered this lifetime, you had a wide range of choices for a physical body. In addition to physical traits, you chose talents and gifts that you inherited from your family line. Some people might say they want different bodies, like the ones of athletes and fashion models, but it's not that simple. The best body for you is the one that gives you the biggest growth opportunities, which does not necessarily match the desirable ones in a worldly sense. Some souls choose bodies that have disabilities or a sickness from birth. Our bodies are meant to give us unique experiences for our growth and the people involved, to serve our growth goals, missions, and desires for physical experiences.

Every family has its ancestors, and from them, you inherited physical traits, as well as mental/emotional traits. For example, if your ancestors went through poverty, you might have inherited virtuous qualities, such as patience, diligence, and collaboration, but you might have also inherited resentment against wealthy people, and a belief that "money is the root of all evil".

In every family line, there are various qualities and beliefs that you inherit as a package. If you are an adopted child, your inheritance is mixed; your physical attributes come from your birth parents' family line, while your mental/emotional construct is a combination of your birth and adoptive parents' traits.

Birth Date, Birthplace, Community, Time of the Planet

A lifepath is not a straight line; rather, it has lots of ups, downs, and cross-roads. There are energy flows that have both a rising and falling momentum. The energy flow of your life is influenced by the energy flow of your environment. The larger the energy, the bigger the influence. One of the things that makes a larger influence in your energy flow is the one from planets, including the Earth, Moon, and other stars in the universe. When you choose your birth date, you choose a particular configuration of influences from the stars, which causes major rhythms and rising/falling momentums in your life. These influences determine the timing of important events, such as difficult challenges, good opportunities, and major crossroads in your life. The detail of influence is well explained by astrologers and numerologists.

Choosing a birth date is closely linked to choosing a birthplace because you will also be influenced by the important events and beliefs of the local community, country, and planet. When you chose a birthplace, you knew what events would most likely happen in that area—economic changes, political situations, wars, earthquakes, climate changes, and so on. In addition, land maintains the memory and energy of all that has happened in the past, and you can pick up certain emotions and beliefs from them. For example, on a land where there was a tragic history, you can pick up sad and depressing feelings. On a fertile land that's had a history of abundance, your feelings will be affected accordingly, helping you attract the same energy into your life. You examined all these environmental conditions and chose a birthplace that worked best for your growth.

Events and Meetings

To fulfill your growth goals and missions, you arranged for certain events to occur in your life. Through these various events, you create situations that push you to grow spiritually. These situations give you challenges and test your virtuous qualities.

A challenge works like resistance training to build new muscle. For example, if you are to cultivate a quality of tolerance, you need a challenging situation that requires tolerance to get through. Some people describe this as "learning from the opposite." Such situations challenge your limiting beliefs and often cause emotional pain. Once you transform those beliefs and heal the pain, you can activate heightened virtuous qualities and move on. If you try to fix a situation on the surface, the situation will recreate itself until you learn the true lesson.

In every situation, there are other people involved, and they might behave in a mean way to you. They are playing those roles to help you experience the situation you need to go through. Often, they also need to learn some lessons from the situation themselves, and all of you agreed to play these roles to fulfill the growth objectives of the group.

Even if you feel that you've learned enough, there is always something more to learn. There are infinite lessons on the path of spiritual growth, and you'll never run out of challenges in life. But as you continue to grow spiritually, these situations become less and less difficult, and eventually, you don't feel challenged at all. In that state, it is possible to always stay in a peaceful mindset, no matter what happens, and you can still find lessons and grow every day.

In addition to challenging events, you as a soul arranged opportunities in your life. Opportunities expand your activities and guide you to the next chapter of your life. Some examples are an opportunity to study abroad, join a new company, move to another city, get married, or have a baby. An opportunity comes into your life when you overcome some important challenges and are ready to move on. Opportunities guide you to the life path you planned for yourself and the destination of your destiny, which will ultimately lead to the utmost joy and fulfillment in your heart.

To support your growth goals and missions, you also arranged important meetings. There are two types of meetings. First, there are meetings with helpers who give you inspiration, advice, direction, messages, teachings, and healing. Do you have someone in your life you would call your role model? That's a helper who is here to inspire you. Do you have someone who listens to your complaints and lets you vent? That's another helper who's here to heal you. The meetings with these helpers are essential for you to stay on track with your path, and you asked them to help you before entering this lifetime.

In addition to helpers, you meet with your promised people. These are the people that you promised to help in some way... maybe by giving advice or demonstrating a good example. Every time you overcome a challenge, you learn a lesson. As a soul, you promised to share your learned lessons with a group of other souls. These people might include your family, friends, customers, students, or audience. If they are not in your life now, they will show up in your life when you are ready. Their souls are waiting for you, and they recognize you when you communicate with them from your heart. Therefore, it's easier to find your promised people through activities or business based on your life lessons. As you share your teachings, you transmit your energy from your heart, and that comes across to your audience and touches their heart in a special way. Then, they will subconsciously recognize you as their helper.

2. DEVELOPMENT PHASES

Adolescence

The foundation for your life path is set over the course of adolescence, establishing the initial trajectory of your entire life. For many, this happens in your relationships at home. You meet your parents and other family members and learn everything from them.

Let's say you wanted to develop compassion in this lifetime. How would you make it happen? To develop compassion, you need a situation that challenges you to develop it. One way to do so might be to be born into a family where your parents or siblings treat you harshly and demand a lot from you. This situation may require you to possess a high level of compassion to accept the situation and dedicate yourself to the benefit of others. Or, another way would be to be born to parents who show you great examples of compassionate behavior you can learn from and embody later in life. Whatever your growth goals and missions might be, you carefully planned your adolescence to set the stage for your entire lifetime. What might be the reason you chose your specific adolescent environment? How did it help you grow?

Family members are the primary sources of knowledge, but you learn from other people too—like friends, teachers, neighbors, TV programs, or even computer games. They teach you in various ways, with gestures, verbal instructions, and facial expressions. Often, people teach others by being an example, both good and bad. Because you interpret these teachings in your own way, there is a lot of room for misunderstandings, and you take everything as "the way it should be." For example, when Dad kisses Mom every morning, a baby will take it as the way a couple should be. Likewise, when Dad comes home from work stressed out and starts arguing with Mom, the child will take that as the norm too.

The teachings range from essential survival knowledge, such as how to eat and how to avoid danger, to social skills, such as how to talk, how to be loved, how not to harm others, and how to form good relationships with others. As a baby, you do not filter any information coming from the environment and simply accept everything as truth. You do not choose which information comes in or out until you form a set of foundational beliefs to make conscious choices from. As such, the first several years in childhood establish the "initial programming" of your life. Note that it is only an initial one; it can be changed later.

These teachings are memorized as a series of programs (beliefs, perspectives, and assumptions) and are used as the basis of your thinking. As a child, your parents were happy with everything you did if it met their expectations. They'd tell you how good a child you were, and you would say to yourself: *of course, they love me. I did what they wanted. I'm a good girl/boy.* You started believing that, to be loved, you had to do what they wanted. Likewise, if your dad was busy working the whole weekend and forgot to go shopping with you like he promised, you'd say to yourself: *he's always like this when he's busy working!* and you would subconsciously accept the belief that work is more important than you. If you watched your parents fight over money, you would probably create a belief that money makes people mad, thereby creating a fear of money situations in your own life.

Using these accumulated teachings as a foundation, you gradually grasp more conceptual yet important ideas, like your identity, values, ambitions, and purpose in life. This knowledge manifests as your thoughts, emotions, behaviors, decisions, and actions, and they all profoundly influence your life experiences. They determine what you like, who you like, how you feel about every situation, how you react or respond, and what you aspire to do in life. The definitions of important concepts, such as success, happiness, love, and good/bad, are also determined by this knowledge.

As there are so many differences in everyone's life environments, some people might compare their life to others' and think it's not fair—and they are right. Our environments are not created equal nor are they fair, and that's fine. You chose your environment because it best serves your growth goals and life missions. Your life environment is prepared just for you, a unique, special, and precious opportunity for you to experience human life and grow spiritually.

Physical Development Phase (Age 0–7)

The first development phase is the primary period of developing your physical foundations, like your skeletal structure, muscles, physiology, and movement. In addition, your parents, guardians, or teachers played vital roles in transferring their energetic programs related to safety, security, relationships, love, money, and abundance. In other words, your life was influenced by those around you during this period. If they did not feel physically safe in their life and were not relaxed in their bodies, you took that in. If they did not have confidence in themselves and felt that life was dangerous and harsh, you took in those beliefs too—beliefs such as "life is hard; I have to be cautious and serious all the time." But if they had confidence in themselves, you took in those programs to enjoy the beauty of being in your body, which enabled you to radiate your inner warmth and shine throughout life. If they felt that life was safe and loving, you took that in, and your body learned to relax and enjoy its natural internal harmony, thereby attracting a life that is lighter, more joyful, and full of opportunities and possibilities.

A young child learns through play. The desirable environment for a child would be a safe, nurturing, loving, and virtuous environment, both in a physical and energetic way. However, not everyone chooses such desirable environments; instead, some people choose challenging ones—chaotic family situations, physical disabilities, turbulent times in society, and so forth. Some of you might have experienced situations that caused severe pain because of extended isolation, neglect, abuse, or molestation. These can surface as problems in the next two phases as you develop emotional and mental capacities. If not handled properly, it is likely to cause serious problems in adulthood, such as empathic distress, people-pleasing, abusive relationships, shame, regret, guilt, and self-punishment. Possible challenges and how to solve them will be discussed in Part II.

One of the most important things you learn in this period is how to be loved. Typically, challenges in romance and marriage can be traced back to your relationship with the parent of the opposite sex. Your behavioral patterns in romantic relationships are likely to be modeled after your parents' or guardians' relationships. As a child, your life is dependent on your parents or guardians, and you need them to take care of you in many respects. As such, your parents' love toward you is crucial to your well-being, making learning how to be loved extremely important for a child. If not taken into consideration, many learn to get attention from others by meeting their expectations, creating this belief that you must meet expectations from others in order to be loved. If parents are not giving attention to a child, a child tends to believe there's something wrong with them, which causes the child to not feel good enough and potentially push to meet their parents' expectations and gain their approval. If not addressed during adolescence, this belief can cause conditioned love in relationships, such as one-sided giving, people-pleasing, or abusive relationships.

What is the condition for happiness? How do you define success? You learn these ideas about happiness and success from people around you in this period, and they drive your dreams, visions, and motivations. These learned ideas do not always serve you well. Your parents might teach you that happiness comes from having a lot of money or fame or a high social status. If you saw your parents fighting over money frequently, you may have picked up negative ideas, like "Money is dangerous," "Money makes people mad," or "Money is evil." These, of course, will influence the rest of your life accordingly, creating a reality exactly as you believe it to be.

The antidote to conditional relationships is recognizing and accepting that there can be unconditional love in your life in the form of relationships where you are loved, understood, respected, and appreciated as you are. It's also important to identify your value and worthiness based on your inner qualities instead of through external achievements or conditions. False ideas about important concepts, like happiness, success, abundance, and life purpose, need to be dropped to discover your authenticity and true purpose in life.

If you had deep challenges in this phase, you likely have had many lessons to activate your virtuous qualities (patience, tolerance, unconditional love, worthiness, and abundance). I imagine your life missions would guide you to help people experience these very qualities in their lives.

Exercise: How to Be Loved

1. Think of the most important and influential person in your life during childhood.

2. Ask yourself:
   What did I need to do to be loved by them?
   How has this relationship dynamic affected my relationships today?

Emotional Development Phase (Age 7–14)

The second phase is emotional development. Experience in this phase could be sweet or painful but never boring. Through this phase, you experience emotional situations with your peer groups and create patterns of how you handle emotions and relationships to form your basic identity. Before arriving at this phase, you learned patterns of emotions and relationships from your parents or others around you, and patterns of how you feel about your physical body. If these patterns are created out of fear-based ideas, they can cause struggles in dealing with situations during this time.

Your experience in this phase is likely to affect your social life in adulthood. Challenges such as social rejection, fear of attack, and low self-esteem can typically be traced back to this period. If you would like to improve your social/work relationships or increase your confidence, this is the period to go back to.

The primary theme in this phase is emotional management. In the previous phase, you might have accepted everything your parents or guardians told you—not anymore. In this phase, you formulate your own opinions, make judgments when your parents or teachers are wrong, encounter conflicts with your peer groups, and experience acceptance or rejection from the opposite sex. These experiences can cause emotional turmoil during this period, and there are two extreme ways of responding to these emotions: express or suppress. If you express your emotions too much, you can hurt others and make it difficult to develop close relationships with others. If you suppress your emotions too much, you can build up negative energy in your body, which can turn into an emotional time bomb or health issues later in life.

Mood Swings

Hormonal changes during puberty make you extremely sensitive to everyone and everything, causing volatile emotional situations. Small things can seem like major disasters. Mood swings are also prominent when it comes to sexuality. You often go through an emotional upheaval when you become attracted to the opposite sex. Acceptance by the opposite sex can feel like heaven, while rejection can feel like the end of the world.

This is an opportunity to learn how to handle your emotions and stop yourself from being trapped by difficult emotions, so you can maintain peace of mind. Unfortunately, the opportunity to learn emotional control is still limited in our societies, and it is common to receive confusing messages about emotions and sexuality. As such, many of us struggle in this phase.

Conflict

During this period, you form basic emotional defense patterns that you carry throughout your adult years, which make your relationships peaceful or otherwise. As you become more sensitive to everyone and everything, it becomes harder to control your emotions, making it difficult to handle conflicts with others. When in conflict, you feel the need to defend yourself from danger. Some choose to set boundaries and push back; others choose to fight. These responses to conflicts tend to cause emotional pains on both parties. What you really need to develop here is emotional maturity. Instead of trying to defend yourself against another party, you should work on stopping yourself from being trapped by your emotions. This is an opportunity for you to learn to manage your emotions, but it will not be easy because not much guidance is available on this subject in today's society. If you don't learn emotional management in this phase, you will have situations that serve as learning opportunities to develop it later in life.

Peer Pressure

In an environment with increased conflicts, who you align with is important. This is the time when you start to form social groups with peers, and accept or reject others based on similarities and differences—gender, opinions, physical appearance, hobbies, and so on. In a way, this experience shapes your ideas about who you are and what makes you unique. You might encounter events that make you feel insecure—like you need to fit in among others in the group. Some might feel compelled to do whatever it takes to be accepted by their peers, even if it means doing things they do not want to do. This can cause pain from not being able to express their true feelings and not being able to stand up for themselves.

In peer groups, subtle differences can stand out among others, leading to teasing or bullying. Bodily differences in puberty present such challenges—being taller, smaller, fatter, or thinner, having a different skin color or hairstyle, and so on. Early sexual maturation can also be a cause for teasing. Even if one is not the target of teasing/bullying, just watching others' experiences or hearing painful rumors about others can be enough to scare you. You might get obsessed with the idea that there is something wrong with you, which can cause you to develop lower self-esteem.

Identity through Comparison

Through experiencing peer pressure, you begin to understand what makes you unique by comparing yourself with others and labeling yourself as "good enough" or "not good enough." Your peers look at you and make their opinions, which also affect your idea of yourself. If they look at you with admiration, you feel you are superior to others. But if they look down at you or even ignore you, you may say to yourself, "people don't like me. I am not normal/appropriate/likable/lovable. I am nothing. I don't belong here." These experiences impact your basic sense of identity.

If you go through the process of identifying yourself through comparison and judgment, you will most likely feel difficult emotions, like jealousy, anger, resentment, anxiety, and despair, because there will always be someone else who is better than you. If this is the case, you will have opportunities later in life that will teach you how to identify yourself through your authenticity.

If you end up identifying yourself as "not good enough," which is a very common belief in today's society, you will lose trust in your ability to navigate life, causing profound worry and fear about what might happen in the future. In an attempt to feel secure, many people try to create peaceful environments by pleasing others, even at the expense of their true feelings and opinions. As a result, they learn to suppress their feelings, losing touch with their authenticity in the process. On the other end of the spectrum, people might express anger quickly and project it onto others, resulting in them pushing others away.

The antidote to emotional challenges is attention control. If you've built up suppressed emotions, they need to be healed and released to prevent emotional explosions or health issues later in life. For healing to take place, you will need to activate virtuous qualities, such as acceptance, understanding, respect, compassion, and forgiveness. All of these will be discussed in Part II.

If you've experienced deep challenges in this phase, you've likely had lessons to activate acceptance, understanding, respect, compassion, forgiveness, honor, and emotional intelligence. People with these qualities make great leaders and fulfill missions to be of great service to humanity as a whole.

Exercise: Conditions for "Good Enough"

1. Think back to your childhood days.

2. Ask yourself:
   What did I need to do to be considered "good enough"?

   What did I do that made me "not good enough"?

   How are these beliefs affecting my life today?

Mental Development Phase (Age 14–21)

If you would like to create more balance in life, activate your creativity, and increase your motivation, this is the phase to come back to. Your thinking abilities develop rapidly in this phase, forming mental structures that your opinions and decisions are based upon. Through acquiring knowledge and various skills, you develop intellect, or the ability to comprehend the objective facts of the external situation. Your spiritual intelligence also starts developing in this phase. It is possible to increase your spiritual awareness and formulate your identity, life purpose, motivations, and vision according to your heart, so you can proceed to the spiritual development phase that immediately follows this one.

For many, this period is full of struggle—building mental faculties, acquiring knowledge, dealing with academic pressures and competition, fitting into peer groups, planning for the future, and addressing unfinished challenges from the previous two phases. Unaddressed emotional issues from the previous phases could get worse here, possibly causing depression, obsessive sexual behaviors, drug use and alcoholism, excessive isolation, and other self-destructive behaviors.

The most serious challenge you might experience in this phase is the dominance of your mental intelligence, which can become so powerful that it takes over your emotional and spiritual functions. Emotional intelligence is responsible for feeling, liking, and enjoying experiences, and spiritual intelligence is responsible for your wisdom, intentions, priorities, and purpose. As your mental faculties become powerful, you tend to put them in charge of your life, allowing them to dictate how you feel, how you behave, what you do, what you want, and what you like or dislike. For example, if you are asked, "what do you want to do today?", the answer from your brain overrides the true answer from your emotional and spiritual intelligence. Throughout adolescence, you've internalized others' opinions about what you *should* do, *have* to do, or *must* do, and these are used as the basis of answers from your brain.

Examples of "Should" Voices:

"As the oldest son, I *should* find a stable job to support my family."

"I *should* get married in my twenties, and that *should* make me happy."

"I *shouldn't* waste my time doing nothing."

Unfortunately, the majority of these "should" ideas are driven by fear, and they are loud in your head! The fear-based ideas are so powerful that they suppress the ideas from your heart. Eventually, you lose contact with your heart and say, "I don't know what I really want." As a result, you formulate your identity, life purpose, motivations, and vision based on what you *should* do instead of what you really want. These fear-based voices tend to drive people to focus on their achievements, therefore investing a significant amount of energy on working hard and winning competitions in their pursuit of "happiness" and "success" as defined by mental intelligence. Other challenges that can arise from subscribing to fear-based ideas include scarcity beliefs, an excessive desire for significance, a comparison-based identity, low self-esteem, self-punishing behaviors, criticism, jealousy, and burnout.

Please note this is not to discount the importance of mental intelligence. Mental faculty is extremely important to comprehend the objective facts of a situation, identify practical solutions, create effective disciplines and habits, and much more. Still, mental intelligence is not supposed to dictate what you feel or what you want in your heart. If your mental intelligence is taking over the roles of your emotional or spiritual intelligences, I bet you will have challenges that serve to help you unlearn those ideas, enabling you to activate your authenticity and identify your life missions.

Reading through the development phases so far, some of you might be wondering why your soul has chosen challenging life environment for this lifetime. If you feel you had a lot of intense challenges in your adolescence, it is because you are a brave soul. You knew what might happen in your childhood, and you still decided it was the environment that best supported you in fulfilling your purpose in this lifetime. To build strong muscles, you need stronger resistance. To bring out your higher qualities, you need an environment that demands such qualities. You chose those life experiences because you knew you could grow a lot through them. You knew you could overcome all challenges and flourish with your highest virtuous qualities later in life.

Whatever life you are living, I suggest you be proud of yourself because you are doing your best in every difficult situation you encounter. It does not matter how your life looks from a worldly perspective. No life is better than another. You are walking a path that is uniquely tailored for you and you alone.

Adulthood (Age 21+)

After going through adolescence and accepting your initial programming, you move on to adulthood. Some people attain a high level of spiritual growth in adolescence and are able to move on to fulfill their life missions early in their lives. However, the majority of us have many unfinished businesses from the first three phases, and continue to address them in adulthood. Some souls choose to get started with their life mission earlier in their life while still addressing unfinished businesses along the way; others choose to do more heavy lifting before getting started with their life mission. Either way is fine. Everyone makes progress at their own pace, and it does not make one life superior or inferior to others. Every experience and every life path is unique, special, and precious.

Just because you accepted your initial programming as a child does not mean you have to live with it for the rest of your life. You can change it at any time. However, people don't usually change their programming unless they have to. The opportunity to change your programming comes into your life when you are challenged and pushed to change; how you deal with it though, is up to your free will. Many programs can be easily changed by simply accepting a different program. Let's say you believed in Santa Claus. One day, your big brother told you it was a lie and that your dad was acting as Santa Claus. As a result, your initially programmed belief disappeared and you accepted a new belief, even going so far as to ask your dad for a Christmas present in the years following instead of asking Santa.

Programs become harder to change when they are charged with emotions, especially negative ones. For example, if your dad becomes busy and doesn't spend time with you for a long period of time, your feelings may get hurt and you may start to believe he does not love you anymore or there is something wrong with you. You may become angry and sad. Your dad might tell you he loves you and that you're a good girl/boy, which makes you feel better for a moment, but when he's busy again, the pain and emotions come back to you, enforcing the belief that there is something wrong with you or you're not good enough. Even when you try to shake off those beliefs and trust your dad instead, you cannot let go of them because you have those painful emotions reminding you and reinforcing the beliefs. As you grow up, these beliefs manifest themselves in your life again and again in other relationships. Whenever you have someone important in your life—friends, a boy/girlfriend, or a partner—you are afraid of losing the relationship. Then, you try to please the other person in an effort to not lose them, often at the expense of expressing your true feelings.

These emotion-charged programs manifest themselves in various situations in life. The situations can sometimes be harsh and painful, but they are always opportunities for you to let go of the accepted knowledge and incorporate new beliefs that serve you better and allow you to grow. To do so, you first need to heal the emotional pain. You need to accept that the old beliefs were not true. Then, you can become ready to accept a new set of beliefs, such as "people love me for who I am. No matter what happens, love stays the same. I am free to express my feelings." When this reprogramming takes place, there is almost always a moment of realization, or an aha moment, where you feel more freedom, energy, and hope in your life.

Your initial programming might cause many of these emotionally charged beliefs, and that's OK! Yes, they cause challenges in life, but you can grow through them, and that is exactly why you came to this game of life. There are many ways to heal emotional pain and change initial programming, but I am going to share with you the way that I found to be effective in later chapters.

Spiritual Development Phase (Age X)

As you make progress in overcoming life challenges and completing unfinished businesses from adolescence, you arrive at a crossroad where you need to choose whether or not you move on to the next phase of spiritual development.

This is an opportunity for you to remember who you truly are, why you came to this lifetime, what you really want in life, and where you are heading. In a way, you are letting go of your old way of life and entering the new, just like the Phoenix that burned its old self and rose from the ashes anew. With this transformation, you activate many virtuous qualities and begin to live your life as an authentic presence.

Dark Night of the Soul

During the path of spiritual development, your biggest fears can cause a period of emotional turmoil that is known in ancient spiritual traditions as the 'Dark Night of the Soul'. It serves as an ordeal in a hero's journey that tests your highest qualities and brings out the best in you. The emotional turmoil is so intense that you cannot turn your back on it. It can come as a burnout from work, a failing business, relationship challenges, or health challenges.

If you are having a Dark Night of the Soul, it means the time is nearing for you to address your life missions. To reach a level of growth that matches what your life missions demand, you need to make a jump. It is like a crash course to finish up many of your unfinished businesses at the same time. To do this, your soul is giving you alone time or solitude, so you can focus on conquering your biggest fears.

Discover Your Phoenix

Upon conquering your biggest fears, you will discover your Phoenix, which is a symbol of your authenticity and awareness of your life's missions. It is the resurrection of your soul and a rebirth into a new life. As you conquer your fears and activate your higher virtuous qualities, you will raise your vibration so much that you will regain access to greater awareness as a soul, where you have clarity of what is important in your life.

At this point, you are no longer driven by survival needs. You will be compelled to be of service to others and help them grow and prosper. That is the state of the Phoenix. Your body, mind, and spirit will be in alignment and will bring out the best version of you, and you will encounter opportunities that lead you to meet your promised people—mentors, allies, and your audience—to fulfill your destiny.

3. UNIVERSAL LAWS

As discussed earlier, the purposes of joining the Game of Life include spiritual growth, contribution to others' growth, and enjoying a physical reality. I believe most of us share these goals. You preplanned challenges that will help you grow spiritually, and you arranged opportunities to fulfill your life's mission to contribute to others' growth. On the other hand, enjoying a physical reality is far more dependent on your free will and your fluency in the laws of the universe. How you experience your life is up to you; you can choose to go through your life lessons with less suffering, experience a lot of happiness and joy, and live a more wealthy and successful life in a worldly sense. Or, you can choose the opposite. Of course, birth environments are vastly different across many individuals and that might give you some initial limitations, but you can still manifest your experience to whatever you wish using the laws of the universe. Understanding these laws and how they work can make a major difference in creating the life you desire.

Law of Vibration

Many years ago, when I moved to New York, I adopted two little kittens, a red and brown tabby, respectively. I remember the very first day I took them to my apartment, they both were nervous and tense, crying out so loud. Out of the cage, the red one started sniffing around the apartment, and I followed him around to see what he'd get into. Shortly after, I realized the brown one

41

had disappeared. I remembered that she ran somewhere once she was out of the cage, but I didn't know exactly where she went. I looked everywhere—below the bed, behind the sofa, around the TV stand—but I couldn't find her. *Come on! This is only a small one-bedroom apartment. How can she disappear here?* Hours later, I finally found her hiding in the tiny space inside the built-in heater on the wall. After I managed to get her out of the heater, she was still nervous and scared, hissing at me incessantly. I had no choice but to put her back in the cage until she got used to being with a human.

Fortunately, the situation completely changed after some weeks. The kitten eventually got used to being with me and made it a daily routine to sleep on her back with her arms and legs stretched out to show her tummy and invite me to stroke her. When I moved closer to her, she looked at me and meowed gently. There was no nervousness anymore. None. She was happy with her life, and was comfortable and at peace. To me, the nervous state of the cat in the beginning felt like she was a totally different being compared to her happy state some weeks later. There was no change in her appearance, but I could feel the clear distinction in her vibe.

In science, a distinction of vibes can be detected as a difference in vibrational frequencies in the electromagnetic field. Nervousness is one frequency and happiness is another. Our inner thoughts, feelings, and emotions are always vibrating and radiating waves. Whatever we think and feel generates waves and travels through time and space. When you are happy, you radiate waves at a frequency of happiness. When you are angry, the waves radiate at a frequency of anger. Have you ever seen an angry person and immediately felt their energy? If the wave of anger is strong, it can affect your feelings so much that you begin to feel it, too. On the flip side, when a baby is happy, smiling, and giggling, you can feel it. It's not just an intelligent understanding of "OK, this baby is happy," but the baby's vibe actually affects your feelings. We all notice the subtleties of different vibrations and say, "I feel good vibes here!"

This is why strong feelings are often contagious. When Martin Luther King, Jr. said, "I have a dream," it was not the words that moved people; it was his passion that was conveyed through the tone of his voice that travelled across the audience and triggered the movement that transformed society. Likewise, many things in our daily lives affect us, too. Do you feel happier when you see beautiful flowers or hear joyful music or the sound of birds? Have you ever felt a feeling of wonder and amazement when you encountered a gigantic mountain? Everything in our lives vibrates and radiates waves, which affects us in different ways.

The effects of strong waves stay in people, things, and lands until they are changed into something else. People feel the energy of past vibrations for a long time. I used to work on Wall Street until a few weeks before the attack on 9/11. Years later, when I traveled back to the place that's now called Ground Zero, a series of different feelings jumped into my heart and over-whelmed me. The energy of the attack and the feelings of the people affected were still there.

We influence our environment with our thoughts and emotions, which are the products of the programs—beliefs, perspectives, and assumptions—we've been taught. Naturally, we are influenced by our environment as well, which includes all the animals, plants, stones, and other inanimate objects; we are all interacting and influencing each other and everything at all times. In this sense, you can never be separate from others; on a soul level, you are connected to everything.

In general, so-called "negative" feelings vibrate at lower frequencies, while "positive" feelings vibrate at higher frequencies. As we all know, our feelings tend to change at random moments, thus our vibration changes at random moments, too. Sometimes we are angry and are vibrating at a lower frequency, and at other times, we are compassionate and are vibrating at a higher frequency. As we grow spiritually and activate our virtuous qualities, we gradually become able to maintain higher-vibrational feelings, such as compassion, kindness, humbleness, tolerance, and acceptance. Therefore, your spiritual growth is experienced as an increase in your vibrational frequency. When you become able to maintain higher virtuous qualities, you will be less influenced by the lower-vibrational feelings of others, such as anger or jealousy. It will be as if you tuned into a radio station with the frequency of compassion and you don't hear anything from other radio stations because they are operating at such different frequencies.

Considering the Law of Vibration, my suggestion is to cultivate your virtues as much as possible. It serves you in attaining spiritual growth, helps you stay away from unpleasant life experiences, and gives you a greater chance of experiencing happiness, joy, and fulfillment in life.

Exercise: Law of Vibration

1. Think of someone in your life who gives off good vibes. What is so special about this person?

2. Then, think of the best moment in your life so far. What vibe did that experience give you?

3. Ask yourself: How can I maintain good vibes every day?

Law of Focus

Many years ago, I had a colleague named Dave. He was a tall, masculine guy with an energizing voice, who was kind to everyone. Every morning, he said, "Morning, Hiro!" and I felt energized and responded to him in the same way. But one day, I noticed he was upset. He received a harsh e-mail that shamed his work and questioned his competency. It made him pretty angry, but instead of responding immediately, he decided to take some deep breaths and wait until the next day.

On his way home, he could not help but think about the e-mail. "Why does no one understand me? Nobody listens to me! I feel like I'm managing a zoo full of angry animals," he thought to himself. When he came home, his family noticed he had a bad day. They felt his vibe. His family was afraid to talk to him because he was so grumpy that night. They treated him like he was a fragile time bomb, and the whole night was ruined. Because his attention was so focused on anger, his thoughts and emotions were affected, and his life experience reflected that energy.

Some days later, he shared his experience of that night with me. I advised him to focus his attention on what he wanted, instead of what he did not want. This made an immediate difference in his life. The next time he received an e-mail complaint, he acted differently; although the same angry feeling came up, he was able to pause and say to himself, "It's OK; I will take care of this tomorrow. Everything is going to be fine. Let's go home and focus on having a happy time with family." With this little mindset shift, he was able to have a good time with his family after a stressful incident at work.

You experience whatever you choose to focus on. To manifest your desired actions and outcomes, you must invest your inner resources, i.e., your attention, thoughts, emotions, and passion. If you focus on your negative thoughts, your manifestation will reflect that same vibrational energy. As great masters say, "Focus on what you want. Stop focusing on what you do not want." Focusing on the positive is how you shape your life in every moment.

Dave learned to shift his attention from what he didn't want to what he wanted fairly quickly, but this is not easy for everyone. Many people get trapped in their negative feelings for weeks, months, or even years. They might be able to shift their attention to more desirable feelings momentarily, but it is hard for them to stay in that space because their negative thoughts and feelings are strong enough to distract them and drag them down. This is why it is so important to build the ability to effectively practice attention control and manage your emotions. With attention control, you can maintain focus on one thing, and let all other thoughts and feelings disappear, allowing you to experience more of what you want in life.

What if we do not make the conscious choice to focus? Our life goes into autopilot. According to neuroscientists, when we are not focusing on something, we are prone to experiencing rumination, mind-wandering, and self-criticism—perhaps, leading to regret about what happened in the past or worrying about the future. These thoughts and feelings are emotionally charged and, thus, are louder in our minds and are strong in trapping our attention. Due to our survival instincts, we are prone to focus on fear-based ideas. Without practicing attention control, it is hard to get out of autopilot.

Attention control is a skill anybody can develop. It is like building a new muscle—a mental muscle to focus your attention at will. Many meditative traditions have practices for attention control. In the past, people used to sit on the mat for hours every day, but easier practices have surfaced in recent years. The most popular practice is breathwork, or taking a few minutes to focus on your breath. Thanks to the increasing popularity of mindfulness techniques, you can easily find guided meditations for attention control on the internet.

Considering the Law of Focus, my suggestion is to focus on what you want instead of what you do not want because that mindset shift can greatly impact your experiences in life. To do this well, you must develop the ability of attention control.

Exercise: Attention Control

1. Close your eyes and focus your attention on your breath. Pay close attention to how your body moves as you breathe in and out.

2. If your attention wanders, notice it and gently bring it back to your breath without judgment.

3. Continue this for at least three minutes, then open your eyes.

Law of Attraction

Energies with the same frequencies synchronize, amplify, and unite for co-creation.

Many years ago, I had a dinner party in the center of Tokyo. I was with a group of friends who practiced meditation together and traveled to interesting places, such as Sedona and Egypt. One lady started talking to me about a healing technique that can change subconscious beliefs using theta brain waves through a short meditation. I felt her excitement and joy, and was fascinated by the possibility of changing my beliefs; so, I immediately signed up for the workshop to learn the healing myself.

The technique in the workshop was very good. I cannot discuss it in this book, but it was simple and fun, and introduced a unique visualization practice that helped facilitate an altered state of mind. It allowed me to experience feelings in my brain I never had before; perhaps, it was the theta brain waves. With that practice, I learned how to change my beliefs and heal my emotions, and the instructor did a demonstration on me in front of the class to remove my fear of heights. *My fear of heights is gone? Really?* I was very skeptical, so one day after the class, I went to one of the top floors in a tall building and looked outside to test myself. I was fine. I went up to an even higher floor of another building, and again, I was fine. I was tempted to talk to my friends about this change, but I still had doubts. *What if I go higher in the building and get scared?* I wanted to prove this once and for all, so I decided to go skydiving, which was a bold move, but that's how badly I wanted to confirm it. With the help of a skydiving school, I got on a helicopter, went to a height of four thousand meters (13,000 feet), and jumped. How was it? It was so fun and exciting! The surge of adrenaline was unexplainably awesome. I felt like I was reborn.

Skydiving gave me proof that the healing technique worked beautifully. I was very excited about the possibilities it could bring to everyone's lives. Many people could change their lives dramatically. I started sharing my experiences with many of my friends and colleagues, inviting more people to try the healing technique. The word spread quickly to many others, and when we hosted a meet-up event, more than a hundred people showed up. All of them were excited about the possibility of changing their lives through this method, and all of us wanted to spread the healing method to others and dreamed about inviting the founder of the healing method, so we could get certified to teach it. This idea quickly became a shared vision of everyone in the community. Every time we got together, the community grew larger and larger. One thing led to another, and we somehow communicated with the founder, and our dream came true; the founder came to Japan to certify people to teach the method.

What happened after that was phenomenal. Many of us taught the method through workshops, and the community kept growing. The founder came to Japan again the next year, and continued to come every year after that. In roughly five years, the healing method became one of the most popular healing modalities in Japan, with hundreds of instructors certified to teach it. We used to say, "Everywhere you go in Japan, you can find workshops of this healing, and you can experience excitement and joy with new friends." The energy of joy and excitement was shared by a large number of people, and it somehow created a huge momentum to make the vision come true. Feelings were transferred through communication, attracting people who shared a vision to take action toward making their dream a reality. It was not a one-person job but, rather, a collaborative effort.

The Law of Attraction became well-known in the early 2000s, thanks to popular books and videos. Some people claim you can manifest what you want just by having a thought, without any action. While I do support this idea as the direction of our spiritual evolution in the future—and perhaps some evolved individuals might have such capabilities today—I don't believe we are there yet as humanity.

The Law of Attraction that is in effect for the majority of us works more on the basis of "good vibes" or "good chemistry." When you communicate with others, your feelings are conveyed beyond language through facial expressions, tone of voice, body postures, and behaviors. People feel your energy and react either in harmony, disharmony, or somewhere in between. How might these reactions affect our feelings?

According to scientists, if two waves are in sync, the energy amplifies to the sum of the two waves. What this means is when you find people who have the same feelings, the feeling amplifies; two happy people make themselves even happier. This explains how like-minded people increase their energy when they get together. When I share my ideas with someone who is like-minded, we get excited and come up with even greater ideas together.

On the other hand, when I talk to somebody who is stressed and not paying attention to me, I feel out of sync with the person and I feel my energy deplete. Have you ever experienced something like that before? If you pay attention to another person, you can feel the difference of their energy, whether it's joyful, serious, boring, or dangerous. It's just like perceiving different colors or sounds. Naturally, we all like to be with someone who shares the same feelings; as the old saying goes, "Like attracts like." The good news is, you can easily attract like-minded people and share great ideas with others, thus bringing in opportunities that can manifest your idea into reality.

The Law of Attraction means you are attracting people and things that match your energy, i.e., your visions, thoughts, emotions, beliefs, and perspectives. By interacting and joining forces with others who have the same energy, you can amplify said energy and manifest your vision into reality.

Exercise: Law of Attraction

1.   Who in your life tends to amplify your good feelings?

2.   Ask yourself: What visions, beliefs, or perspectives do I share with this person?

Law of Time & Space

In high school, I took on a heavy course load so I could enter a good university, but sometimes my mind wandered away from my classes and fantasized about other things. I used to imagine hanging out with my friends and playing basketball, having ramen together, or even going to the moon or other galaxies. My mind was liberated and unlimited, flying across the sky, going to the future, past, and anywhere else I could imagine. After a while, I found myself brought back to the present moment, still in the classroom. Have you ever experienced something like that before?

You can experience your body only at a single point: here and now. But in your mind, you can go to any time and space as long as you can imagine. The question is can you change what happened in the past? Yes, you can. Well, you cannot change physical and material aspects of what happened in the past, but you can change energetic aspects—like your thoughts, feelings, emotions, beliefs, and perspectives about the situation.

Let me give you an example. Many years ago, when I was working in a corporate job, I had a colleague named Harry, and we had a good, trusting relationship. We used to run important projects together, often working until late at night to solve difficult problems and going out for dinner afterward.

He used to express gratitude to me in front of everyone, and I did the same. One day, the company's executives asked me to make a short presentation about our project and explain how the team worked toward the same goal. After the presentation, I received an e-mail from Harry, who was very upset about my presentation.

"Why are you presenting it like it's all your achievements? It's my project, too, and you should have asked me beforehand. Who do you think you are?"

His response shocked me, and I got upset. In my mind, I said, *what's wrong with him? He did the same thing with our projects before, and he didn't ask me beforehand. Nobody does such a thing. He is the one who's selfish!*

I didn't want to respond with anger because of the chance it might lead to an intense argument. In hindsight, I should have tried to clear whatever misunderstanding there was, but I didn't. I just wanted to calm down and regain my peace of mind. I felt attacked, judged, and denied. Something in my heart was torn apart. I tried my best to calm down and focus on something else so I could forget the incident. Harry and I continued to work on projects together, but our relationship changed. We were distant and cold toward one another. I behaved calmly and professionally on the surface, but I was still angry inside. Whenever I saw him, I felt negative emotions come up, which stressed me out. I could physically feel it as a burning sensation inside my stomach.

Years later, when I was learning the healing technique, I realized I still hung on to that anger. Whenever I encountered somebody that reminded me of him—people who attacked, judged, and denied me or others—I felt the same negative emotions that caused the burning sensation inside my stomach. What happened in the past affected me in the present moment physically, emotionally, and mentally. I was afraid that the physical sensation might turn into a sickness someday, so I decided to do something about it before it became a bigger problem.

How did I solve the problem? It might have been easy if Harry apologized for what he did, but I knew that wouldn't happen. He had already left the company, and we had lost contact completely. So I turned my attention to myself, to change the energetic part of what happened in the past, to heal the pain and let it go.

This is possible because of the Law of Time and Space. You only live in the present moment physically, but you can go to any time and space energetically. This means you can change the energy of any time or space in your life, be it the past, present, or future. The energetic change you make in the past will be reflected in your energy in all other times and spaces—and physically at the present moment. You can change your life today by changing your feelings about the past.

To create my energetic changes, I first looked back on the past moments and noticed all the feelings, emotions, beliefs, and perspectives I experienced with Harry. I felt attacked, judged, and denied by what he did, and after realizing that, I asked myself what I wanted instead. I wanted to be accepted, understood, and appreciated. I asked myself what I learned from the experience. I learned never to allow others to affect my feelings and ruin my life again. I learned how to stop my desires for acceptance so I could experience peace, no matter what others might say. I imagined listening to myself in the past, the younger me who was confused and angry, and saying, "It's OK; you're safe. I am here for you, and I love you. I accept you, understand you, and appreciate you." I imagined my younger self becoming liberated from the anger, and I imagined myself letting go of all the feelings that no longer served me. Then, something interesting happened. A feeling of compassion started to arise within me. Harry is only human. He's also learning to be a better person, and he makes mistakes sometimes just like me. He wants to be happy and free from suffering just like me. I wish for his happiness, and I forgive him.

What happened? The burning sensation in my stomach disappeared. When I thought about Harry, anger no longer came up. I felt like I could talk to him again as a colleague without any hard feelings. I might not trust him like I used to, but I could see him with compassion.

The world inside your mind is a world of energy based on your initial programming. In your mind, all time frames exist at the same time. You can change how you think about your pain from the past. You can change not only your feelings today but your worry about the future as well. This way, you can create happiness and empower your physical body today. Just remember what happened in the past, heal the pain, and reframe it with a new perspective and meaning.

We will talk more about how to change your energies from the past to impact the present day in the 'Challenges and Opportunities' chapter.

Exercise: Law of Time & Space

1. Think of a challenge that has repeated in your life. What situations do you find yourself in over and over again?

2. Ask yourself: What is this trying to teach me?

Free Agency

Let's say you have a son. After graduating from college, he started his own business but got into trouble with one of the suppliers and ended up with a lot of debt. He came to you devastated and not ready to deal with the situation. What would you do?

A. Pay off his debt with your money.

B. Call the supplier and negotiate for him.

C. Offer advice and support for him.

If you're in this spot as his parent, you might be tempted to do A or B. Perhaps you have the money or negotiation skills to make it work. But these don't do anything for your son. Remember, we all came here to experience challenges and grow. This situation was created by his "I am" consciousness, as a growth opportunity. This challenge helps him bring out his higher qualities. Paying off his debt and conducting negotiations for him would take away a precious opportunity for his growth, and if you do this every time he gets in trouble, he will become dependent on you. Instead, you need to trust that he can bring out his strength and capability to overcome the situation by himself. This is not easy; it takes patience and compassion on your end. You can still offer advice and support by mentoring or coaching him so he can recognize his inner capacity to overcome the situation, but it does not serve him well to take his place and do the work on his behalf. You cannot grow for him, just like you cannot build a muscle for him. When a person goes through a big challenge, the resulting growth is big, too. As the saying goes, "What doesn't kill you makes you stronger."

When I was ten years old, I had a painful incident. I was attending class at elementary school, and when the teacher asked me a question, I didn't understand what she meant and couldn't answer the question at all. Then, the teacher started humiliating me in front of the class, blaming me for not focusing on the lesson. I felt everyone judging me and attacking me. I cried. I felt pain in my heart. Since then, I've had a fear of speaking in public and have avoided such events as much as possible.

Even after I graduated from school and started working, I still had the fear. My job required me to do some public speaking, and I always felt challenged and nervous, not able to do a good job of it. When somebody says they're afraid of speaking in public, people often tell them to just keep doing it until they get used to it. I did that, but it was like I was forcing myself to ignore my nervousness, and I was still not able to enjoy speaking in public. Eventually, my responsibilities expanded in the company, and I had to speak in front of bigger audiences; I felt pushed into a corner. I had to face this fear and let it go. So I decided to take time to work on it.

After some digging and contemplation, I remembered the childhood event at the elementary school when I first felt judged and attacked, and I realized it was the cause of my fear. Then, I turned my attention to my classmates. I remembered how they watched me during the event, but I also remembered how supportive they were afterward; they were angry with the teacher for how she treated me in front of the class, and some of my friends actually confronted the teacher for me. They were not judgmental or critical; they cared for me. This was a wonderful finding.

Then, I turned my attention to the teacher. I remembered her facial expression, which was nervous and almost fearful, not the kind of expression usually made out of anger. At that moment, I realized it was not about me. There was something going on in her life, and she was not behaving as her true self at that moment. When I became aware of this, I started to feel sorry for her and my deep-seated resentment turned into compassion. I felt the hard feeling in my heart melt away. Feeling better about the event, I turned my attention to what I could have done differently. What if I maintained my confidence, was OK with making mistakes, and was graciously open to feedback from the teacher? The whole event may have been a positive experience for everyone. By being such a presence, I could have empowered everyone in the class. This thought brought up a new energy in myself. It is not about how people look at me and how I can look good in public, it is about what I can do to empower others, possibly even inspire them, for the better.

Through this contemplation, I was able to drop my fear of being judged and attacked by others, and instead, I activated compassion and the intention to be of service to others. This realization changed my feelings about public speaking dramatically. I became excited about the next opportunity for public speaking, and I was no longer nervous. Since then, I've started to enjoy public speaking, bringing my passion to inspire others.

My fear of judgment was something I created in childhood, and it contained precious lessons for me. Nobody could take that away from me. That is the Law of Free Agency. By working on resolving the energetic memory from the past, you can change the energy and apply it in the present moment. Others cannot take over your learning opportunity for you, but you can ask for their support. You can ask your friends and family to guide you in examining a life challenge and deciphering what the lesson might be in it.

In every life challenge, there is a hidden agenda for growth. Once the growth is attained, the challenge gets resolved, and the person moves along the path to the next opportunity. If you know someone who's going through a challenge, you can offer your help and support if the person asks, but be careful not to violate their path for growth. Who makes the call? The person as an "I am" consciousness. If, by any chance, your help violates their agenda for growth, the person will need to experience a similar challenge again. The situation might get resolved on the surface, but the need for growth will remain in the energetic reality, causing another challenge to show up so the person can complete the lesson. This is why many people go through the same challenges again and again, whether it's a difficult boss at work, miserable relationships, a big loss in business, or any other challenges in life.

4. REALIZATIONS & IMPLICATIONS

After years of meditations and private sessions, I had a moment when I was finally able to connect the dots and grasp the idea of the Game of Life Theory. This was followed by realizations that liberated me from the fear of uncertainty and increased my faith in myself, my life, and God. Now, how does this theory help us live a better life? I believe it helps us experience the greatest amount of joy and fulfillment.

Let me summarize some of my important realizations that have changed the way I live my life.

Seven Realizations

1. **Quest toward God**

   We are souls born from God, and each of us is on a long journey of remembering and experiencing our God-inherited qualities, which we typically describe as virtues. Human life is one way to make progress on this journey.

2. **Growth, Contribution, and Experience**

   A human life gives us opportunities to grow spiritually, contribute in other people's growth, and experience God's qualities in the physical realm. I believe these are the primary purposes of our lives.

3. **Every life is special, precious, and important.**

   There is no one way to fulfill these purposes. Any life experience gives us the opportunity for growth. It does not matter how much wealth, fame, or success we have in a worldly sense, and this is not a game that has a winner or a loser; it is not a race or competition because you are the only one who is walking your particular life journey.

4. **Challenges are gifts in disguise.**

   Challenges in life are opportunities to grow spiritually. There is always a lesson hidden in every challenge. When you complete the lesson, the challenge resolves by itself, and these lessons help you demonstrate more of the virtuous qualities you inherited from God, thereby revealing your authenticity.

5. **Healing is essential.**

   When we experience a challenge, sometimes our feelings get hurt and we experience emotional pain. To overcome a challenge and turn it into an opportunity, you need to heal that pain, let it go, and fully learn the lesson. Later in this chapter, I will share with you how I heal this pain.

6. **Joy/Fulfillment**

   There was a time I kept asking for the difference between joy/fulfillment and happiness/satisfaction during meditations. The answer I received was that happiness/satisfaction are related to physical experiences, while joy and fulfillment are related to spiritual experiences, meaning joy and fulfillment are feelings we experience as souls. Activating our authenticity and completing our life missions give us such experiences.

7. **Happiness/Satisfaction**

Experiencing happiness and satisfaction is as important as experiencing joy and fulfillment. How much you experience happiness and satisfaction depends on 1) how well you work with the universal laws to create what you want in the physical reality; 2) how you refine your learned conditions for happiness/satisfaction; and 3) how well you manage your emotions. The previous chapter about the universal laws should help you with number one, and the upcoming chapters about challenges and opportunities should help with numbers two and three.

Dark Night of the Soul

Sometimes we experience a big challenge that drags us down to rock bottom. It flips our lives upside down and makes us feel like everything is falling apart. You might feel your life is done, but this is the moment where your greatest transformation is about to take place: your resurrection from the Dark Night of the Soul. Let me share my experience and how I overcame it.

Years ago, I looked down from the balcony of my fifteenth floor apartment and thought it might be easier if I just ended my life at that moment. My important relationships were falling apart, and I had run out of options. All my prayers went unanswered. I felt ignored, rejected, and abandoned. It was excruciating to go through such uncertainty, and it made me feel powerless, helpless, and worthless. Day and night, I was alone. I had work-related phone calls and meetings, but I was not able to share what I was going through with them. I felt nobody would understand. There were days I didn't talk to anyone. I was obsessed with thinking about worst-case scenarios and got so insecure. I tried to meditate and heal myself with everything I had learned until then, but I couldn't go to the calm, peaceful state I usually went to during meditation. I struggled. It felt like there was no way out, and the emotional turmoil seemed to last forever.

It's amazing what those emotions could do, though. As I look back, my life back then was not that bad; it was good. My healing activities and businesses were all going well. I was abundant financially and materialistically. There was only thing that was not working well: my relationships. But those dark emotions were powerful enough to make me think everything was falling apart. There was a part of my mind that kept telling me, '*relax, you're just fine*', but those voices were blown away by my dark emotions in seconds.

The emotional turmoil didn't go away. It lasted hours, days, and weeks. Even a sunny day with blue skies seemed like a dark night to me. No wonder. Later, I found out this experience of intense emotional challenge had a name: Dark Night of the Soul. Since ancient times, it has been well-known in many spiritual traditions, and there is no easy remedy but to make a leap in spiritual growth somehow and break free from those emotions. In fact, the spiritual leap is the real purpose of this emotional challenge, according to spiritual traditions. But I could not find any instructions on how to make the leap.

I felt that I had hit rock bottom. I was lost. But I didn't want to give up. I was open to trying anything to recover. First, I needed to stop the dark emotions from distracting me. Usually meditation helped with that, but as I could not even meditate, I decided to try some different tactics, like going for a run, eating nice food, and so on. Then, I found one thing that worked well: singing. When I sang a song that resonated with my emotions, which was usually a sad song, those feelings gradually became less intense. It was as if I was getting the emotions out of my body simply through the tone of my voice. I felt better after singing for some days—enough to be able to meditate again. It still was not as easy as it used to be, but I continued meditating every day. Some days later, I felt a voice come from my heart: "*Hiro, you're OK. You're safe. I am here for you. I love you. You're not alone. Just accept who you really are.*"

When I received this, I felt like I was being touched in my heart for the first time in a very long time. I felt safe and protected. This gave me a relief, and I was able to breathe deeper. During meditation, I simply kept focusing on my breath, breathing in and out. Gradually, I was able to calm down and rest in a peaceful state of mind. I still had many negative thoughts and emotions inside me, but I was becoming able to dissociate from them and keep a mental distance from them. I watched them like they were objects or energies stuck in my body. I felt the dark red energy of helplessness in my heart, a heavy, dark blue sadness in my lungs, and a black despairing energy in my stomach. As I watched them and identified them as energies with color, it got easier over time to distance myself from them.

After a while, I heard another voice from my heart: *"Go inside."*

There was nothing to lose. I gave it a try. As I imagined going inside the helpless feeling in my heart, I remembered the first time I felt it in my life. I was fourteen years old, and I had a crush on a girl in school. When I asked her out, she said no, and it felt like the end of the world. In my imagination, I watched the boy, my younger self. He looked so helpless.

The voice from my heart said, *"Listen to him."* I imagined listening to the boy. He was sad and didn't understand why things didn't go as he expected. It was as if he could not control anything in his life—like he was powerless. He figured there must have been something wrong with him, that nobody loved him, that he was alone.

The voice from my heart continued, *"Embrace him."* I imagined myself hugging him and said, *"You're OK. You're safe. I am here for you. I love you. You're not alone."*

Something changed at that moment. I felt something stuck in my heart begin to melt away. The emotional pain became a little better, but it was still there. Then, I heard the voice again:

"What did you learn from this?"

I remembered I used to hang out with the girl in a group; it was always me, her, and another girl who was her best friend. As a group, we had a lot of joyful conversations. Then, I realized I put her in a difficult spot. If the two of us became a couple, it might end up leaving the other girl alone, and she might have lost her best friend. I understood she chose to maintain our friendship as a group.

So, what did I learn from this? I learned that I had to respect her decision. It's not that she hated me; she wanted harmony with everyone together. It's not that I was alone; even though I couldn't date her, I had two good friends to have joyful conversations with.

With this new perspective, I realized all the negative beliefs my younger self told me were just misunderstandings. They were all proved wrong. Instead, the opposites were true; I do have control over my life, I am lovable, and I am surrounded by people who love me. Gradually, I felt the last pieces stuck in my heart get washed away completely, and eventually, the painful feeling disappeared.

I was so glad I found a way to let go of that intense emotional pain in my heart, so I moved on to the black, despairing energy in my stomach, and repeated the same process, and it worked well. After that I moved on to the next and the next, and after several days, I was able to let go of everything, all the emotional pains I could find in my mind and body. They all disappeared! And I retrieved the following lessons (and many more) from them all:

- I am connected with everyone and everything.

- All I need is within.

- God is always supporting me.

- I deserve to be loved fully and completely.

- My worthiness stays the same, no matter what others say.

Then, something amazing happened. I finally experienced the absence of all negative emotions. Have you ever experienced an absence of negative emotions in your mind? I thought it would be a flat, neutral feeling, but that was not the case. The moment all the negative emotions disappeared from my mind, I experienced extreme happiness. It was like there was a beautiful, morning sunshine inside of me. I believe it was the feeling called "bliss". For many days, I could not help but laugh and smile. I was so happy, really happy.

Emotional Healing

After recovering from my Dark Night of the Soul, I shared my experience on social media and started helping others overcome their emotional challenges. The process that helped me heal my pain proved to be effective in others, and I discovered more processes and tools to support different emotional situations.

There are three keys at the core of emotional healing: Attention Control, Embracing, and Reflection.

Attention Control

To manage your emotions, you need to get out of the illusion of your emotions and observe them from a distance. A practical way to do so is with attention control, as discussed in the Law of Focus section. This is a skill you can develop through training, such as mindfulness. If you are new to attention control, try the exercises I introduced in the previous chapter. You can start with just a few minutes a day. Although it is recommended to continue practicing attention control every day for years, you can begin to distance yourself from your emotions easier in just a few weeks.

Embracing

When you become able to observe emotional pain through attention control, you can start healing it. If you dig deep into your emotional pain, you'll find that the root cause is often fear—fear of losing love, fear of death, fear of becoming nothing, and so on.

The most effective antidote to fear is love. To facilitate healing this pain, you must give love to it.

- First, think back to the moment when the emotional pain originated and look at yourself as you were then.

- Then, let your past-self tell you everything and just listen. By listening, you are giving attention to them, and attention is a form of love. This begins the healing process.

- After they finish talking, imagine hugging them, and give them words of love. I always use the same phrase I received in my Dark Night of the Soul experience:

"You're OK. You're safe. I am here for you. I love you. You're not alone."

Embracing is an act of love. It facilitates healing of the emotional pain and empowers your inner self to get out of a fear-based illusion. Notice how the feelings change as you take this step.

Reflection

The final step is to retrieve the lesson from the challenge. The way to do this is through reflection, which is an important psychological exercise that can help you grow, develop your mind, and extract value from your mistakes. Reflective questions prompt you to review the past situation deeper, identify lessons learned, and reframe the meaning of what happened in the past— possibly leading to an important realization. This is the step that gives you closure and allows you to move on with renewed energy and increased motivation to live your life better.

There are many questions you can ask yourself in this step, and each works well for different situations, but the most common and useful ones are:

- What did I learn from this?

- How did this help me grow?

- What virtues did I develop through this?

In Part II of this book, I will introduce the most common challenges that show up in many people's lives, and I will offer some guidance, tips, and reflective questions to facilitate emotional healing. I hope you can enjoy this journey of healing and empower yourself as you read this book.

To further aid in your emotional healing, you can take advantage of a technique called Phoenix Blessing™ through workshops and videos. Using a series of visualizations and reflective questions, you can heal your emotional pain, change your beliefs/perspectives, and empower yourself to increase the joy and fulfillment in your life.

Visit my website https://www.phoenixblessing.com for more details.

Part II:
CHALLENGES AND
OPPORTUNITIES

I n Part I, we discussed the Game of Life Theory, universal laws, and the challenges that come with each development phase toward discovering your Phoenix. When you decided to join this game of life as a soul, you knew all the possible joyful experiences, as well as challenges that might happen, and you knew what you'd grow up to become in adulthood. You might wonder why our souls wanted to do all of this. I believe it is for the evolution of our souls. Every soul is on its journey to return home to the consciousness from which all souls were born. People give different names to it—the Big Bang, the Great Unknown, Something Great, Creator of All That Is, God, and so on. We inherited all the highest qualities from the origin, but they need to be recognized, experienced, and embodied. The human Game of Life gives us precious opportunities to make progress in our journey. Upon activating your authenticity and life missions, you turn yourself into a Phoenix that rises fro m the ashes of old and becomes an agent of transformation for others.

A majority of us carry unresolved issues or unfinished businesses from our adolescence and continue to address them in adulthood. Each of us goes through various challenges in life, which are growth opportunities in disguise. To overcome each challenge, we must unlearn some beliefs and perspectives that no longer serve us and cultivate higher qualities.

Let me share with you how these challenges might show up in your life.

Turning Challenges into Opportunities

Have you ever wondered why you're often faced with the same challenge again and again in your life? Ever wonder why a problem does not resolve quickly and makes you feel miserable for a long time? Chances are these situations were caused by unfinished business from the past that's trying to teach you something. Once you retrieve a lesson from the challenge and recognize your growth, you will gain a new perspective that enables you to overcome the situation, and your emotional pain will be healed. Then, and only then, can you move on. By doing this, you've turned the challenge into an opportunity to create more happiness, joy, and fulfillment in life.

A client of mine named Tamara was very stressed when she called me for help. Her husband cheated on her again, and she had already decided she would leave him, but she was troubled by the fact that she'd been cheated on in many of her past relationships. She wanted to find out what the real cause behind it was.

She said, "I cared for my ex-partners and did a lot to make them happy, but nobody really ever treated me as 'number one' in their life. They always had something more important than me, and I was at the bottom of their priority list. Why is it always like this? They made me feel betrayed, miserable, insecure, and small. Maybe it's me. I am not a good girl, not good enough, not lovable."

I asked, "When was the first time you felt those feelings in your life?"

"It was with my dad when I was little—around five years old. He was a very charming man, kind, gentle, and joyful, but he broke a lot of promises that he made to me—things like buying me a dress for a party, taking me to a national park, or coming to my graduation ceremony. These were important to me, and we picked a date and time to do them, but there was always something more important coming up, and he stood me up. I thought I had to do something to receive more attention from him, so I worked hard to meet all his expectations to prove myself. I performed very well at school, and I took good care of my younger sister. And yet he kept breaking promises. I felt betrayed, miserable, insecure, and small," she said.

Listening to her, it was obvious the situation with her dad in adolescence was repeating in her adult relationships. She had been carrying the pain of being betrayed by someone she loved and created beliefs that she was not good enough. This pain must have attracted the kind of men that provided her with that same situation so she could heal the emotional wound. She needed to heal the pain, drop the belief, and identify with her higher truth to change the pattern of her relationships.

Hiro: I would like you to imagine yourself talking to who you were as a five-year-old girl. What did she want from her father?

Tamara: She wanted him to give her more attention. She wanted him to look into her eyes and hug her. She wanted to know he loved her.

Hiro: Ask her why he didn't give that to her.

Tamara: She says it's because he didn't love her. There was something wrong with her. She was unlovable. She was not enough to be loved.

Tamara started crying. She remembered the painful feelings she felt back then.

Hiro: Do you think these things are true?

Tamara: No. It was his problem. He was distracted and careless. There was nothing wrong with me as a child.

This is an important insight. It was not her problem; it was his problem. Even though her father loved her, he didn't know how to love his daughter in a way that made her feel loved. Just like everyone else, her father needed to learn some lessons. Children interpret their parents' behaviors in their own ways and often create negative beliefs about themselves. That needs to be changed.

First, Tamara needed to heal this five-year-old girl—the part of her consciousness as a child.

Hiro: Tamara, I need you to do something. Imagine coming closer to your five-year-old self and hug her. Hold her in your arms. And say, "It's OK. You are safe. I am here for you. I love you. There is nothing wrong with you. You are lovable, and you are more than enough to be loved." How is she reacting?

Tamara: She is … better. She is relieved and peaceful now.

Hiro: How do you feel?

Tamara: I feel warmer in my heart.

Now that she felt some peace, she needed to complete her lessons by acknowledging them and creating a new vision for her life going forward.

Hiro: How did this experience make you grow as a person?

Tamara: I became stronger and patient. I became a responsible person, and I learned to do everything by myself, but as a result, I cannot receive help from others. I learned to care for others, but often at the expense of my own needs.

Hiro: Imagine the most desirable situation possible. You have all these good qualities, including strength, patience, and dependability. You can take care of yourself, fulfill your needs, and love yourself. And you can also receive help from others and make your life even better. You enjoy loving others and being loved by others. What are you noticing now?

Tamara: It's wonderful! I feel happy!

Hiro: How is that five-year old girl reacting to this?

Tamara: She's so happy! She's dancing around.

Hiro: Silently say to yourself, 'This is in my life now'.

Tamara: Yes.

Hiro: How do you feel now?

Tamara: I feel good! And I am confident that I can find a happy relationship now.

This child in her imagination was a part of her consciousness that had been stuck in a cycle of painful emotions for a long time, still looking for attention and love. She had been trying to heal this pain through her romantic/marriage relationships, but of course, she had been choosing people who had similar lessons to learn as her father. In fact, nobody could be the perfect parent or partner who could always be with her, heal her pain, and love her unconditionally except for one person: her. She is the only person who knows herself inside out and could love her and give her everything she needed. By talking to her five-year-old in her imagination, she could pay attention to the voices of the pain she had been carrying for a long time, and she could heal herself and move on.

During this session, I also discussed important topics, like worthiness, compassion, and self-love, with Tamara. She realized her worthiness was eternal and magnificent just for being who she was, and that it never changes, no matter how others treat her. What happened was unfortunate, but it was caused by their problems, not hers. She deserves to be loved fully and completely by a partner who treats her as the highest priority in his life.

During the discussion, I saw her shoulders loosen and release tension, her face relaxed and lit up with a smile, and her breathing slowed. She was able to liberate herself from the emotional pain, increase her self-esteem, and gain clarity and confidence in what she wanted to experience in her relationships going forward.

Guess what happened after the session?

First, her anger and disappointment toward her past relationships disappeared. She no longer regretted what happened in the past, but she acknowledged how she grew through it all. Second, she promised to focus on loving herself and allowed herself to receive help from others. She stopped trying to do everything alone, and started seeking help from others, and giving herself plenty of time to rest. She listened to her heart more and did all she could to enjoy her life.

Shortly after, she met the man she had been longing for, a man who always made her his number one priority, giving her help and support while fully respecting her opinions and decisions. With this man, she felt loved and was able to experience the joy and happiness of sharing her life with somebody who appreciated her for who she truly was.

What happened to her was not just a resolution of a problem, but more of a transformation into an authentic individual. She turned a challenge into an opportunity to transform her life and created the happiness she was longing for.

If you are experiencing a challenge, there is something profound hidden in it that will give you an opportunity to transform your life. In the pages that follow, I'll share with you some of the common themes that happen in our lives.

Seven Stages

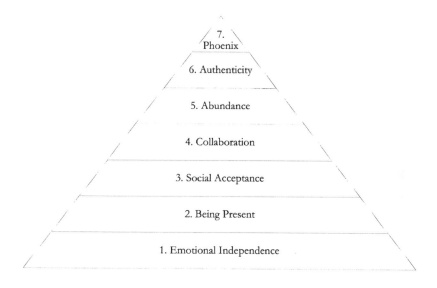

Stage	Challenge	Opportunity
1	Emotional Dependency	Emotional Independence
2	Living in the Past or Future	Fully Alive at Present Moment
3	Victim of the Environment	Leader to Create Change
4	Competition	Collaboration
5	Scarcity	Abundance
6	Uncertainty	Authenticity
7	-	Clarity of Life Mission

From numerous private consultation sessions like the one with Tamara, I found there are common themes of challenges that everyone goes through in life, and I categorized them into seven stages. You might be going through one of these stages now, or perhaps, multiple stages at the same time. Stages 1 through 5 are focused on your spiritual growth, and increasing your happiness and general quality of life. These can happen one by one, or altogether.

The order of occurrence can be backwards too. Stages 6 and 7 are focused on transforming yourself into the state of the Phoenix with activated authenticity and an awareness of missions to create the utmost joy and fulfillment in life.

I'll begin with a brief overview of each stage, and then, we will go into greater detail.

Stage 1. Emotional Independence

Emotional dependency means your emotional life is affected by others. This is connected with empathy, a heightened ability to understand what another person is experiencing emotionally. Empathy is good, but if you experience others' emotions as yours, your emotional life will constantly be affected by others, making it difficult to create peace and happiness in your life. This can also lead to a desire to please others at the expense of your own needs, or control others so you can create peace in your environment. By overcoming emotional dependency, you can take full control of your emotional life and experience peace of mind and happiness every day, which is essential for activating creativity.

Stage 2. Being Present

In life, we all experience challenges or failures. Each such event causes emotional wounds. Every time you have a similar experience, you remember the painful emotions from the past, and it drags you down. You lose confidence, suppress your capacity, and lose the opportunities in front of you. However, these challenges in the past are not meant to disempower you; they are meant to teach you something and help you grow. The painful emotions are a reminder for you to retrieve the lessons and let go of the past, so you can live fully in the present moment.

Stage 3. Social Acceptance

In ancient times, humans had to belong to a group to protect themselves from predators and engage with mates to create future generations. In those days, when it was very dangerous to live by oneself, social rejection was equal to a death sentence. Times have changed, and there is far less physical danger now, but an experience of social rejection still triggers various negative feelings, such as anxiety, insecurity, anger, sadness, depression, and low self-esteem. These feelings hinder your ability to change the status quo for the better and cause a victim mentality. By overcoming these feelings, you can liberate yourself from the prison of social pressures, activate your creativity, and transform yourself into a leader who introduces a new way of life to the society.

Stage 4. Collaboration

When severely defeated in competitions, people give up on themselves and allow fear to rule their life. They feel powerless and hopeless, and become depressed. They put themselves in a victim mentality, spending their life complaining, whining, and self-pitying. Even if you tend to win competitions, a competitive mindset is tied to a fear of failure, and it can make your life miserable. By overcoming the fears and getting out of the illusion of "survival of the fittest," you can turn this into an opportunity to redirect your life toward a higher purpose. As you conquer the fears and release the desire for significance and superiority, you will be able to participate in competitions with a totally different energy. Your intention will be to increase your level of excellence in an effort to bring out the best version of you. With this mindset, a competition becomes a collaborative effort to bring out the highest possible expression of everyone involved.

Stage 5. Abundance

Abundance is the mindset that there is more than enough of something to activate the highest qualities in yourself, others, and everything around you.

It is a way of life that embraces and appreciates all that exists in the world, knowing there is more than enough for everyone and everything to express itself at its highest potential. What prevents you from experiencing abundance is fear. Fear takes away your virtuous qualities and activates the worst version of you, triggering negative emotions. By seeing high qualities in everyone and everything, including yourself, you can experience joy in every moment, and attract people and things with the same high-quality energy.

Stage 6. Authenticity

In life, you'll be met with a crossroad where you'll need to make a choice between diverting to a new path and staying on the same one. The new path is a journey toward authenticity, to connect with your heart's desires and live your mission of life. This is a calling to adventure; it shakes your belief system and triggers fears. There are lots of uncertainties and your brain will probably scream, "No way!" At the same time, you will feel an unexplainable urge to take the new path because your heart knows it will trigger a metamorphosis, and help you flourish into an authentic being. You can still ignore the calling, pretend that it's not important, and overwhelm yourself with other things, but life will never give up on you. It will keep bringing it to your attention until you finally take on the adventure.

Stage 7. Phoenix

As you follow your heart and live as an authentic being, you will gain clarity on what you really want in life and how you can be of the best possible service to others, which will ignite your passion to invest in something greater than yourself. This is the state of the Phoenix. Everything that happened in life prepared you for this, and you will activate your highest gifts, talents, and capacity to fulfill your missions, and you will experience the utmost joy and fulfillment.

STAGE 1. EMOTIONAL INDEPENDENCE

Ann had a pleasant day. It started with clear blue skies and gentle sunshine, and she enjoyed a nice latte with her colleagues at a café. She performed well at work and received recognition in public, and she enjoyed constructive and joyful conversations with her boss and colleagues. She came home with such a happy feeling. However, when she opened her apartment door, she heard her husband yelling on the phone, obviously upset about something. After hanging up the phone, he started talking to her about what happened in his business and how his clients were treating him harshly, expressing his anger and frustration. She understood what he was going through and started to feel frustrated as well. In addition, his tone of voice was intense, and it made her feel insecure. Her happiness was gone. She even felt sorry for him and could not talk about how pleasant her day was. She became frustrated and insecure for the rest of the day.

When she came to me, she was upset with everything that was happening in her husband's life and said, "Hiro, can you help my husband in this session?"

She wanted me to help change her husband without him knowing it. I said, "No, I don't have such an ability, and I don't think I should do that, even if I had that ability. But I can help you change yourself, so you're not affected by your husband's emotions, and can stay happy regardless. That'll help your husband, too."

Emotional dependency is when your emotional life is affected by others. This represents empathy, a heightened ability to understand what another person is experiencing emotionally. But if you experience others' emotions as yours, your emotional life will constantly be affected by others, and it will become difficult to create peace and happiness in your life. This can lead to a desire to please others at the expense of your needs or control others so you can create peace in your environment. People with emotional dependency tend to be very smart, efficient, and effective. They can read between the lines and are capable of doing many things by themselves, driven by the need to go beyond expectations. Therefore, many of them earn the trust of their family, friends, and colleagues. On the other hand, after many years of suppressing their feelings and opinions, they may lose contact with their true feelings and won't know what truly makes them happy and fulfilled.

Now, let's go back to Ann's situation. Here is how we found the root of her problem.

Hiro: How do you feel about the situation with your husband?

Ann: I feel frustrated and insecure.

Hiro: When was the very first time you felt these feelings?

Ann: I know when it happened for the first time. It was with my father when I was around six. He was always angry and frustrated about something and yelling at my mother, and sometimes they got into harsh arguments. I was scared. I did all he told me to do—even more than he told me to do, so I would not upset him.

Hiro: Did he ever hurt you?

Ann: Not physically, but verbally, yes. When I did something well, he treated me well, and I felt relieved. But when he didn't like what I did, he got upset and yelled at me. I was scared and cried a lot, then he would get even more upset. He was sensitive to behavioral issues—how I looked at him, the tone of my voice, my use of words. I always had to understand how he was feeling.

Hiro: If you can imagine talking to yourself back then, what would she tell you?

Ann: She is scared. She says he's dangerous.

Hiro: What does she want instead?

Ann: She wants peace. She wants to be hugged.

Hiro: What does she need to do to create peace and be hugged?

Ann: She needs to make him feel better with her behavior and by doing whatever he tells her to do.

Hiro: Then he'll hug her?

Ann: Not really. But she can avoid intense situations in the family.

Hiro: And if he was not happy with her?

Ann: He would yell at her and sometimes put her outside for hours. She is very scared of it.

First, Ann needed to heal the six-year-old girl that was still inside her.

Hiro: Ann, I need you to do something. Imagine coming closer to your six-year-old self and hugging her. Hold her in your arms. And say, 'It's OK. You are safe. I am here for you. I love you'. How is she reacting?

Ann: She is crying on my chest. She is feeling more secure now.

Hiro: How did this experience make you grow as a person?

Ann: I guess I learned to understand others' feelings and help them feel better. Not just understand but feel their pain as mine. I have been doing this with others in my life, too.

Hiro: Why did you need to experience their pain like yours?

Ann: I guess... that's how I loved them, and they loved me for that.

Hiro: Would you like to change this so you don't need to experience their pain to help them?

Ann: Sure, that would be nice!

Hiro: OK. Let's create a vision for that. Imagine your husband being stressed and frustrated in front of you. You understand his pain, but you are maintaining a calm and peaceful mindset. You have a clear boundary between your feelings and his. And you have genuine intentions to alleviate his suffering. What are you noticing about yourself?

Ann: It's an interesting feeling... sort of a new feeling for me. But I see it's possible. I feel peaceful and calm, and I feel I can help him better this way.

Hiro: What are you noticing about him?

Ann: He appreciates my understanding of his feelings and is grateful for my intention to help him.

Hiro: If you show this vision to the six-year-old girl, how does she react?

Ann: Oh, she's so happy! She's breathing deeply and smiling.

Hiro: Excellent. Now, silently say to yourself, 'This is in my life now'.

Ann: Yes.

Hiro: How do you feel now?

Ann: I feel good! That heavy stressful feeling is gone now!

After the session, she started noticing the difference between her husband's feelings and hers, and became able to maintain her peace, calmness, and happiness inside. Interestingly, he felt her inner peace and calmness, and it helped him calm down as well. This enabled her to have more constructive conversations with her husband about his situation, which allowed her to help him better, just like she had visualized during the session.

Emotional dependency is formed early in childhood when you needed to depend on your parents and guardians for nurturing, survival, security, peace, and happiness. As a newborn baby, you just needed to cry out loud to receive what you wanted. As you grew, you learned how your actions and behavior influenced what you received. Sometimes you received happy and loving affection from others, and at other times, you received feelings of disappointment, worry, fear, and anger. As a child, your parents are the most important people in the world. It is important for your survival and well-being to be loved by them. Gradually, you started to look for what your parents wanted from you, and you tried to meet their expectations as much as you could. When you noticed your parents experiencing difficult feelings, you did what you could to alleviate their suffering.

When they are not happy with what you do as a child, it is a big problem. When they say you are a bad girl or a bad boy, you get deeply hurt. As a child, you take everything your parents say or do as the truth. When they say you are ugly, you accept it as a true statement, and it becomes your belief about yourself. When your parents treat your brother or sister better than you, you think there is something wrong with you. When they are verbally or physically abusive to you, you justify their behavior—"I have to be punished because there is something wrong with me," or "They will love me again if I do what they want me to do."

Some children realize early on that they get others' attention and are treated well when they become sick or are suffering from pain. As a result, they start using it as a tactic for attention. I had a client who remembered faking a sickness to get his parents' attention. He also used this tactic to stop his parents from fighting. This is a dangerous pattern. If the child continues to do this, it could become a habit to look for something wrong with themselves. As we discussed earlier, what you focus on, you get more of. The habit of looking for what is not working will bring exactly that, and it does not allow you to fully experience and appreciate what *is* working in your life. You might have experienced these situations with someone other than your parents—like your grandparents, guardians, siblings, teachers, or friends in your neighborhood.

The underlying cause is the fear of losing love. We need love from our parents more than anything else. It's vital to our survival and well-being as a child. As you remember your childhood days, what did you feel you needed to do to be loved by your parents? If you had an experience similar to this, you might have created beliefs that caused emotional dependency, which affects your relationships and job performance today. If you look at the bright side, I bet you also developed virtuous qualities, such as empathy, patience, and perseverance during your childhood. What qualities did you develop?

The only problem is these good qualities were conditioned out of fear, sadness, and anger. Let's rewind your memory through visualization, heal the emotional scars, and decondition your good qualities from unfavorable emotions and beliefs.

Exercise: Deconditioning

1. Think back to a time in your childhood when you were fearful, sad, and/or angry.

2. Listen to what your younger self wants to tell you.

3. When they finish, embrace them with a hug. Notice how your younger self's feelings change and how you feel different.

4. Now, imagine pushing a red button that deconditions your good qualities from all the unfavorable emotions and beliefs.

5. Ask yourself: "What would motivate me to demonstrate good qualities instead? To help somebody? To be the best I can be? Or, to be who I truly am?"

6. Imagine how those good qualities will make you feel. Finish by saying to yourself, "This is in my life now."

As you read, you might be tempted to blame your parents. Please don't. All parents love their child without exception, at least at their core. But parents are humans. They are going through their own challenges in life, and there are many things that can trigger their emotions and behaviors. It is not an easy job to raise a child, and they probably did not know what to do. It is possible that they were raised in the same way by their parents. They might have inherited beliefs from their upbringing about how to treat children. I guarantee you they love you at their core. Also, as children, we sometimes misinterpret our parents' behaviors and languages. Chances are they were going through their own dramas, and it had nothing to do with us. They did their best to not express their emotions in front of the children, but often, such attempts did not work well because children can pick up on their parents' emotions beyond language and take it personally or interpret them in their own way.

The unfavorable behaviors and actions of our parents do not reflect their true nature. They are also travelers on a human journey, just like you. They are not the ones to be blamed. It is their beliefs, fears, and emotions that are to blame.

Drop any negative emotions you may have against your parents or guardians through visualization and forgive them for whatever they did to you; forgive yourself for not being able to stand up for yourself. Note that this does not mean their actions or behavior was OK; you do not need to justify nor agree with them. They have to learn their own lessons and correct their actions and behavior, but you are not responsible for them. You do not need to be involved in correcting them. By forgiving the other person, you can liberate yourself from the anger and move on.

Exercise: Forgiveness

1. Imagine yourself in childhood, facing your parents back then.

2. Let your child-self say everything she/he wanted to say to your parents, all the painful feelings, what she/he wanted instead—everything.

3. When they're finished, urge your child-self to say, "I forgive you. And I forgive myself for putting me in a difficult spot. By forgiveness, I liberate myself from this emotion."

4. Notice the energy difference in your heart.

5. Ask yourself: What do I want instead in my life?

Empathic Distress

For people who are emotionally dependent, it becomes second nature to connect with others and understand others' needs and expectations. It helps them establish a rapport and trust their relationships. However, many of them tend to feel others' emotions so vividly—as if it is their own emotions—thereby joining the experience of others. When somebody is happy, they experience happiness. When somebody is feeling sad, they too experience sadness. The emotion they pick up from others does not disappear; it stays with them until they somehow process it internally and let it go. Unfortunately, not many people know how to process negative emotions, and these negative emotions can build up as they continue to experience others' emotions every day. This causes emotional distress. This is a particularly serious problem for people who are involved in caring professions—like medical professionals and social workers.

These days, people are connected online, and many of our interactions take place without physically seeing the other person. Empathy is an essential quality to connect deeper with others and establish trusting relationships. By overcoming empathic distress, these empathic people can utilize more of their caring nature and promote understanding, respect, and support in society.

By overcoming it, empathic distress turns into compassion. According to Buddhist teacher Joan Halifax, compassion is defined as "the capacity to be attentive to the experiences of others, to wish the best for others, and to sense what will truly serve others." Scientists discovered that people use different parts of the brain for empathy and compassion. Empathy uses the pain region of the brain, while compassion uses pro-social regions. As a result, compassion triggers lower stress (cortisol) responses to stressful social situations.

To overcome empathic distress, you need to do two things. First, you must dissociate from your emotions or mentally distance yourself from them. This is also known as attention control, which I've previously discussed. Second, you must set healthy boundaries between you and others. You do not have to take on others' pain to help them. They have to deal with their emotions, not you. And I bet the other person doesn't want you to go through that pain; they just want someone to care. If you put yourself in distress, you have less capacity to care for another person. You must maintain a sense of calm and peace in yourself while listening to somebody's misfortune. Only then can you offer help to them without sacrificing your well-being. Let's address this through visualization.

Exercise: Setting Boundaries for Others' Pain

1. Think of someone in your life who is suffering from emotional pain. Observe their pain from a distance, while keeping your heart in a calm, peaceful state.

2. Say to yourself: "This is his/her pain, not mine."

3. Then, shift your attention to your intention—to help the person alleviate their suffering.

4. Then, ask yourself: How can I be the best support for him/her to alleviate their suffering?

Over-Sensitivity

When I was managing a project management office in my corporate days, Ken joined us as a project manager. He was a big, muscular guy and was very energetic. As a project manager, he was passionate in driving his project team to achieve the expected outcomes for the company. He usually behaved nicely, but when his emotions got in the way, his attitude was offensive; he often raised his voice, made big gestures, and caused conflicts with his team members that hampered the success of his projects.

As a project manager, he created a project plan and presented it to his team members. Generally, he made a good plan, but sometimes one of his team members gave him constructive feedback to make the plan even better. This was usually when Ken got angry. He didn't take criticism well, and often got frustrated, starting an argument with the person and ending up in a huge conflict where somebody needed to step in. After a few of these incidents, I asked him, "Why don't you take it as constructive feedback and incorporate it into your plan?" He replied, "They are blaming me! They have to change their attitudes first." He was taking the feedback as a personal attack on him, which triggered his anger.

This was a red flag to me. He was putting himself in a victim mentality, and he didn't understand that he needed to change. Countless times, I saw people perform poorly at work, and the majority of those incidents were rooted in their personality traits, which were caused by their beliefs, perspectives, and emotional wounds. Ken was one of them. As his manager, I needed to sit down with him to find out how to prevent this from happening again.

Hiro: Tell me again, how do you feel about the situation?

Ken: They are blaming me. They are mean.

Hiro: What makes you feel they are blaming you?

Ken: Well, they made objections to my project plan and told me to change it. You know, the plan is based on what they told me in previous meetings. They should have told me beforehand. It's their mistake.

Hiro: Did they tell you it was your mistake?

Ken: No, but I didn't like the way they brought it up. From the look in their eyes and the tone of voice, it was obvious they were attacking me personally.

Hiro: Ken, this is not the first time you had serious conflicts with your project team members. This does not help the project or the company. You cannot change other people, but you can change yourself. Are you willing to work on yourself to avoid similar situations from happening again?

Ken: OK, sure.

Hiro: When was the very first time you had similar angry feelings or felt blamed or attacked?

Ken: You mean, in my life? I think it was my father and big brother when I was a small kid. They criticized me, denied me, and rejected me for everything I did, no matter how well I did it. I felt attacked by them all the time.

Hiro: And what did you do when they denied you?

Ken: I got angry, and I fought back. I denied them, and we had a lot of ugly arguments, sometimes physical fights.

Hiro: What were you protecting by getting angry?

Ken: What do you mean?

Hiro: Let me ask in a different way. What would you lose if you didn't get angry?

Ken: I would have lost my place in the family… sort of my significance and comfort in the family. It's like I'd become small and insignificant.

Hiro: What happens if you become small and insignificant?

Ken: People leave me. Nobody loves me. And I become alone. I guess I was afraid of becoming alone.

Hiro: I see. What did you want from your father and brother instead of criticism?

Ken: I wanted… understanding, acceptance, and support. I wish they acknowledged what I did right and encouraged me to improve what I didn't do right. I knew I wasn't perfect, and I wanted them to accept me for who I was.

At this point, Ken was calming down. Anger seemed to have vanished, and he was experiencing emotional pain instead.

Hiro: Ken, I need you to do something. Imagine yourself back when you were fighting with your father and brother, and hug your younger self. Hold him in your arms and say, "It's OK. You are safe. I am here for you. I love you. You are special, precious, and important. You are loved for just who you are." How is he reacting?

Ken: He is crying. But he is OK. He is happy crying. He seems to be relieved.

Hiro: How did those experiences as a child help you grow as a person?

Ken: I got stronger. And I learned to work harder to make good results. That's how I got good grades at school and achieved success at work.

Hiro: Very well. Now, how do you feel?

Ken: I feel easy in my heart. The anger is gone. I see that I do not need to be angry.

Hiro: Excellent. Would you like to create a vision for a desirable relationship with your colleagues going forward?

Ken: Yes.

Hiro: Imagine the moment when you felt blamed during the recent project meeting. Imagine your project members being grateful for your work and really wanting to help you succeed. Can you imagine that?

Ken: Yes.

Hiro: Now, imagine they are giving suggestions to the entire project team, not to you personally, with pure intentions to achieve the best out of the project. They really want to contribute to the company. What are you noticing?

Ken: I feel... OK. I see they are not attacking me, but they are more like, "Let's do this together." I like that. I feel we are working together as a team.

Hiro: Awesome. Now, if you show this vision to your younger self, how does he react?

Ken: He's happy and relaxed. He is motivated.

Hiro: Excellent. Now, silently say to yourself, "This is in my life now."

Ken: Yes.

Hiro: How do you feel now?

Ken: I feel good. I understand I reacted unprofessionally in the meeting. As a project manager, I have to take responsibility for that and fix it by myself. I need to focus on collaborating with the team better for the same vision and goals.

That day, Ken spoke to his project team members individually and apologized for his unprofessional behavior. Afterward, he was able to take feedback constructively and seemed to enjoy project meetings more than ever before.

Over-sensitivity is when people are sensitive to how others treat them and get easily emotionally triggered. For example, when your partner doesn't respond to your text message quickly, how does it make you feel? What if you don't get a response for a day, a week, or a month? With over-sensitivity, it might trigger difficult feelings, like anger, sadness, insecurity, betrayal, abandonment, and so on. In a different scenario, people can get easily offended when people disagree with them. They take disagreements as a threat, attack, rejection, or disrespect. It is just an opinion. Everybody can have their unique opinions without needing to agree with each other, and we can still maintain good relationships.

However, with over-sensitivity, people make their opinions part of their identity and connect it with their worthiness, therefore feeling threatened by others' disagreement. Sensitivity is beneficial in detecting potential threats and helps in understanding others' emotions and needs; however, when it's connected with one's identity and worthiness, it can cause difficult emotions and even trigger fight-or-flight responses.

To avoid creating a difficult situation from an emotional reaction, notice when you get emotionally triggered, then take a deep breath, and pause for a moment. This gives you a chance to calm down and consciously choose what to do next instead of automatically reacting to the situation. This ability to notice your emotions can be harnessed through attention control exercises, which simply involve closing your eyes for a few minutes and focusing your attention on your breath. This might not be easy, even for a few minutes, but as you continue to practice it regularly, you will have better control over your emotions once they arise.

Attention control helps people avoid creating difficult situations from emotional reactions, but it does not prevent these emotions from arising. It is the person's beliefs and perspectives that cause them to interpret others' words and actions as a threat. Overly sensitive people tend to identify their worthiness based on external evaluations, like how others look at them, what they say to them, and how they're treated. When somebody is giving them constructive feedback on their ideas, they take it as an attack on their worthiness, even when the feedback is on the ideas and not the person. They believe their worthiness is determined by others, but that is not true.

The truth is, their worthiness—and everyone's worthiness—will never change, no matter what happens, because worthiness resides inside ourselves. There are inner resources in every one of us, the virtuous qualities we carry from birth. To believe in this, you need to feel that there really is something invaluable and eternal inside you.

Exercise: Feeling Your Truth about Worthiness

1. Imagine that all the doubts, fears, negative thoughts, and emotions are dark clouds floating in the sky.

2. Behind those dark clouds, there is always sunshine. Imagine going beyond those clouds to find the beautiful sunshine.

3. Ask yourself: What does this sunshine represent about me? In other words, what virtuous qualities are hidden behind your dark emotions?

Can't Say No

Elena is one of my healing colleagues, who lives in eastern Europe. She is a gifted, successful healer, and has many clients and students who benefit from her talents. She manages a team of healers and assistants who support many people in their healing.

However, when she got started as a healer several years ago, she was exhausted and asked me for help. Back then, she was already providing powerful healing, and the number of clients who came to her was growing. Every day, she had several private sessions. Healing sessions gave her joy and happiness, and she was grateful for the opportunity to witness healings every day. However, people started contacting her during the night, asking for help. Knowing they had urgent issues, Elena responded to them and often did healing sessions late into the night. Gradually, such "emergency sessions" increased, and it resulted in her working day and night, and losing sleep. Even though healing was a joy for her, the workload was becoming too much, and she didn't feel she could continue any longer. But she couldn't stop; she couldn't say no to those requests for nighttime healings.

Ever since she was a child, she had always said yes when people asked for her help. That made people happy, and they appreciated her kindness, but underneath it all, Elena was afraid of what might happen if she said no. She feared hurting others' feelings and losing their love; people might disrespect her, stop appreciating her, and leave her for another healer. She said to herself,

"I have to bear with this and do everything I'm asked." I advised her to find somebody to help her manage her calendar and respond to clients' requests, so she could have a good work-life balance, or she could hire another healer to work with her so she could handle the increasing number of client requests. She was not comfortable asking for help from others, and said, "I have to do everything by myself."

As we dug deeper to identify the root cause of this mindset, she remembered her childhood days. Her parents wanted her to do everything for herself, in addition to taking care of her younger sister. She did her best to do everything, but it wasn't easy to take care of both herself and her sister, who was running around all the time. When her parents were satisfied with Elena, they hugged her and treated her well, but if they were not satisfied or if she resisted or disobeyed their expectations, they scolded her and locked her in a closet for hours. It was dark and small inside the closet, which scared her tremendously. Over the years, this happened several times, and she learned to obey her parents because she didn't want to be locked in the closet again. This experience must have taught her good qualities, like patience, compassion, and independence, but these qualities were conditioned with the fear of rejection, punishment, and losing love. In her subconscious, she believed she had to satisfy others' expectations and do everything by herself to earn love, respect, and peace.

This conditioning might have helped her in some ways during childhood, but she didn't need it anymore as an adult. Through discussion, she realized she deserved to be loved and respected without needing to sacrifice herself, and it was OK to protect herself, set boundaries, say no, and receive help from others. She could live her life being loved, respected, and appreciated by people she could trust and share joyful experiences with. But there was one thing she didn't understand.

"Why did my parents treat me so harshly? I really don't understand," she said. I guided her to imagine talking to her parents' souls and asking them why. When she came back from the contemplation, she shared with me what she received.

"They are sorry about what happened. They loved me unconditionally, no matter what I did, but they didn't know how to express love in different ways because their parents did the same to them. They want me to let go of this pain and live happily," she said.

Her eyes were full of tears. With this awareness, she was able to let go of the pain from her childhood and cancel her fear-based conditioning.

When I met her again some years later, I was amazed by how much she had changed her life. She was still giving private sessions, but she managed to limit her work day to just a few hours, and she was able to spend more time teaching healing techniques to her students. She found some healers she could trust and formed a team to respond to clients' healing requests, relieving her of the need to sacrifice balance in her life. She learned to use help from others and had several staff members working for her to expand her teaching activities to more cities, reaching a lot more people than ever before. Even in the middle of such expansion, she had plenty of time to experience the joy of helping others, relax, and enjoy her life. I was so happy to see her energized, motivated, and fulfilled.

There are many people who go through this challenge of not being able to say no. They tend to be in a care-based job or position, and they are good at their work, but they often lose balance in their life and become exhausted. If you have this challenge, consider the fear-based conditioning that was created in your past, identify what good things you've learned from it, and make a conscious decision to cancel the conditioning and live your life differently going forward. You *can* create balance in your life. You *can* be loved, respected, and appreciated by others. And you *can* receive help from others.

Exercise: Receiving Help

1. Imagine a group of people who love you, respect you, appreciate your work, and are willing to help you.

2. Imagine yourself being able to relax in their presence, trust them, and openly receive their help.

3. Imagine yourself having clarity about what you want and communicating it to others with ease.

4. Ask yourself: What might become possible with their help?

Micromanagement

Micromanagement is a side effect of emotional dependency that occurs when people are put in a position to manage others. I've observed many micromanaging people during my corporate days, especially new managers. Let's take Steven as an example. As a manager, his job was to assign different tasks for his team members to complete. However, this was not easy for Steven; he was promoted to manager because of his good performance, and he could not bear low-quality outcomes from his team members. He was not comfortable with pushing back deadlines to allow his team to fix their mistakes, so he tried to fix them by himself. This was the reason he always worked so late.

As Steven's supervisor, I told him to stop trying to fix things by himself, and instead, give the work back to his team and let them work on it again. He understood this and started doing it, but after some time, his team members began to complain about his micromanagement. Steven did not trust his team; he wanted to examine the progress of his team's work every step of the way and created rules and procedures for everyone to follow. When a problem arose, he would look into every detail and give detailed instructions. His intention was to prevent mistakes and produce high-quality work, but behind his intention was a fear that did not allow him to trust others to fix their own mistakes. This discouraged his staff and took away their flexibility, creativity, accountability, and growth.

I discussed this with Steven and identified another fear. Being a manager, he had to step back and support his team to produce an outcome, but this made him feel insecure. He felt as if he was not able to contribute like he used to, and he was afraid his staff might produce better results than he did in the past. He was afraid of losing his significance in the company.

Underneath micromanagement is a strong need to meet expectations, distrust in others, and a fear of losing significance. As a child, Steven remembered how demanding his father was, and how he didn't give him any room to make mistakes. He also had an experience of being scolded by his father because of someone else's mistake, and it made it difficult for him to trust others. He realized he was able to establish good discipline, diligence, and integrity because of his father's teachings, but he didn't want fear to drive those good qualities. The good news was he didn't have anger or resentment toward his father. With awareness of how all these things were connected, he consciously decided to let go of the need to meet others' expectations and his fear of losing significance. He gradually learned to trust others in his team and support them in performing their best without micromanaging them.

I met him again several years later. He became a senior manager in the same company, and he had hundreds of people under his supervision. It was proof that he had been doing a great job trusting his staff and delegating his responsibilities while leading the organization to excellence. He said, "Hiro, I remember you helped me when I was a novice manager. I struggled and put you in a difficult spot. But thanks to your help, I was able to learn what it means to be in a management role. Now, I feel joy in watching people grow and shine, and supporting the company to prosper."

Abusive Relationships

It is always so nice to see happy relationships—smiles on people's faces, eye contact, joyful voices, big hugs, the innocent voices of children. They radiate such a sweet energy and make me feel so happy and warm just from being in the same space; it's as if I'm resting in a beautiful hot spring in the countryside of Japan. When people are in challenging relationships, we can also feel its power—a blaming look in their eyes, fierce tones, and their emotional distance. Even worse, I sometimes see tremendous emotional pain on their faces, as they try their best to somehow maintain peace. What is keeping them in such a miserable relationship? Why don't they just walk away?

Kristine was in a relationship with Tony. He was very confident and had strong pride regarding what he did and what he believed in. He loved her and took good care of her, but when she had opinions different from his, he talked about his opinion until she managed to change the subject. She didn't feel the need to decide which one was right and wrong, and she realized it was OK to have different opinions, as each side had its pros and cons. She hoped to enjoy these types of discussions, so they could learn from each other, but he didn't take their differing opinions well. He was obsessed with proving his point, picking out logical flaws in her opinions and demanding that she accept his opinion and apologize. If she didn't do so, he got upset and pulled back into his space. He'd stop talking to her for days—even weeks—until, finally, she gave in and apologized.

After that, communication went back to what it used to be—smiling, active, intimate, and fun. However, when the same thing happened again and again, Kristine started questioning if the relationship was real. "Are we just faking it on the surface? Are we suppressing real feelings?" As she contemplated and searched for true feelings, she recognized some painful emotions she kept inside. She had been trying to forget what had happened, but those memories never disappeared; everything was still deep inside. She spent more time contemplating their relationship and went deeper into her true feelings.

Then, she discovered that, for a long time, she had been feeling disrespected, rejected, denied, ignored, and abandoned. It was not really about the opinion; it was the way he treated her that mattered.

She blamed herself for turning her back on those emotions for so long, and for allowing him to psychologically abuse her. She decided to confront him about this to demand understanding and respect from him. Again, he didn't take it well, and this time, he raised his voice and tensed his muscles to keep himself from exploding. She felt threatened, got scared, and gave up on it, somehow fixing the situation and creating peace on the surface. After that, every time he talked about his opinion, she didn't dare share her own. She was aware that the relationship was getting worse, but she didn't know what to do. She was trapped by the fear of being threatened by her partner and could not stand up for herself. She did not want to go through a scary situation like that again.

When I met Kristine, she looked pale and sad. She was not sure if there was anything she could do with the relationship.

Hiro: How do you feel now?

Kristine: I am tired, Hiro. And I feel disrespected. I feel so small and worthless.

Hiro: When was the first time you felt disrespected in your life?

Kristine: It was with my older brother, George. He was arrogant and violent. He was mean to me. He yelled at me for nothing, hit me on the back, and punched me on the face. I had bruises.

Hiro: Did you tell your parents?

Kristine: My parents didn't do anything. They didn't believe what I said. They wanted a boy and treated George like a prince. They spoiled him like that.

Hiro: How did that make you feel?

Kristine: I felt like I was nothing. I was not important, I was worthless, and I was unlovable because they treated me like a doormat. They disrespected me and ignored me. I was sad, hopeless, and powerless. Insignificant. It was like I was not wanted, like I didn't belong there.

Hiro: Kristine, I need you to do something. Imagine talking to yourself back when you were going through the difficult experience with your brother. What does your younger self want to tell you?

Kristine: She is so sad and scared. She is crying. She says nobody protects her.

Hiro: What does she want instead?

Kristine: She wants someone to really look at her, listen to her, and care for her. She wants warmth.

Hiro: OK. Kristine, I would like you to imagine coming closer to the girl and hugging her. Hold her in your arms and say, "It's OK. You are safe. I am here for you. I love you." How is she reacting?

Kristine: She is feeling better but not sure if she can trust me.

Hiro: Then say, "You can trust me. I will never leave you. I protect you and stand up for you." How is she reacting now?

Kristine: She is hugging me back. She is relaxed.

Hiro: Very well. Kristine, how did that experience as a child make you grow as a person?

Kristine: Perhaps, I learned to be patient and humble. I learned to respect others' opinions.

Abusive relationships vary in their intensity, but the underlying issue seems to be the same. The abuser lacks respect and trust for the abused, causing mistreatment, intense jealousy, controlling behavior, or physical violence. It makes the abused feel miserable, disrespected, rejected, denied, ignored, and abandoned, creating emotional pain. Emotional pain takes longer to heal than physical pain, and it has a serious impact on the beliefs and values of the abused; they often feel insecure, insignificant, worthless, powerless, hopeless, and undeserving of love or happiness. They often blame themselves instead of the abuser. These beliefs and values disempower the abused, and they eventually lose the confidence to create the life they wish for themselves.

Almost all these cases can be traced back to childhood experiences for both the abuser and the abused. Perhaps they were raised in environments where their parents did not listen to children and forced their ideas onto them. Or perhaps, they saw their mom suffer from an abusive relationship with her husband. They felt emotional pain by watching their parents and built up fears in response. For the abused to stop the pattern of abusive relationships, they need to heal the pain from their past by identifying and accepting it and letting it go. They need to learn to stand up for themselves so they can change the situation for the better. For the abuser to stop perpetuating these relationships, they first need to want to change. Once they become open to change, they also need to heal the pain from their past, identify their values, and develop their inner spiritual qualities.

Exercise: Healing the Abused

1. How did you feel when you experienced abuse for the first time? Go deep into the feeling and try to remember exactly how it felt.

2. Imagine listening to yourself back then. Let her/him talk about all their feelings, thoughts, and emotions. When they're finished, embrace him/her with a hug.

3. Tell her/him, "I am here to protect you. You are safe now." Notice how different your heart feels.

4. Ask yourself: What did I learn from this?

Unable to Stand up for Self

Let's continue with Kristine's story.

Hiro: Now, what do you need to feel listened to, understood, and respected by others?

Kristine: I need to confront them. I need to stand up for myself. But to do so, I need to be brave. I need to have courage and strength.

Hiro: Who might be someone you admire that has such qualities?

Kristine: Rose, my boss at work. I admire her, and she has all these qualities and more.

Hiro: Excellent. Imagine Rose is walking into your body. Feel her bravery, courage, and strength in yourself.

Kristine: Yes, I can feel it.

Hiro: Imagine how you would behave in the situation with your brother with these qualities. What do you notice?

Kristine: I am standing up tall. I confront him and tell him he should never treat me bad. I feel I can stand up for myself.

Hiro: Good. Now, imagine your partner, Tony. What would you do in that situation with these qualities?

Kristine: I am determined to push back on him. I tell him my feelings and demand him to change, or I leave him. I know I deserve to be respected and loved. I know I deserve a better relationship. I know who I can ask for help if he gets upset and I am ready to walk away from him.

Hiro: Good. Now, imagine the most desirable relationship. It can be with Tony or somebody else. What do you notice?

Kristine: I have a man who loves me for who I am, and listens to me well. Even if we have different opinions, he respects my opinions and supports me, and I do the same for him. We learn from each other, grow together, and we are so happy.

This is beautiful.

Hiro: Awesome. Now, silently say to yourself, "This is in my life now."

Kristine: Yes.

Hiro: How do you feel now?

Kristine: I feel stronger. I feel confident, and I can stand up for myself.

In abusive relationships, the abused feels there is nothing they can do, so they stay in the miserable relationship. They try to accept it as "just the way it is" and give up on taking any action to change the situation. Because of the pain they experienced either in the current relationship or in past relationships, they cannot stand up for themselves and confront the abuser. By not speaking up for themselves, they avoid going through the same pain they had in the past, but this approach does not solve the situation at all.

Abusive relationships cause a victim mindset, which is when the abused sees their life being controlled by somebody else and believes they have very little say in the matter. They feel overpowered by the other person and often feel the need to give up their desires. They might feel weak, small, and powerless, that their life is the result of their environment and they cannot create what they want in life. Once a victim mindset becomes your mental habit, you always look for reasons why you cannot do things in your life, blaming somebody, a system, or an environment. You lose your creativity and resourcefulness, and spend your time complaining, whining, and being jealous of others. Of course, a victim mindset is only an illusion, and none of those thoughts are true. Nobody has control over your life but you, and you have all the inner resources you need to create the life you want. By recognizing your strength and standing up for yourself, you can take back control and get in the driver's seat of your life.

Another thing involved with abusive relationships is the fear of losing love. Because many of the abused have lost their self-esteem, they are afraid that if they lose their relationship, they won't be able to find another. They tend to believe that their current relationship is the one and only love they can find. They suppress their feelings and lie to themselves by behaving as if everything is fine. Because it is painful to face their true feelings, they learn to ignore them and end up losing touch with their authenticity. The fact that they cannot change the situation makes them feel powerless, small, and insignificant.

Beautiful memories from the past can also prevent the abused from standing up for themselves. Because of the beautiful, sweet moments they had with the abuser in the past, they stick around just in case they come back.

They say to themselves, "If I give up my needs this one time, we can bring the beautiful moments back again. He will love me more and treat me better. If I swallow my feelings, we can create peace and maintain this love." However, this wish won't come true. You can't experience happiness in an abusive relationship. If you need to keep suffering and give up your needs just to stay in a relationship, how can you be happy? If you lose touch with your feelings, how do you know what you really want in your life? You deserve better, and you can create happiness by yourself. You have that power inside you. To do so, you first need to stand up for yourself. You need to bring out your strength and courage to confront and change the relationship. That way, you can take control of your life and be its creator instead of its victim.

To be released from the trap of this illusion and stand up for yourself, you need to heal emotional wounds from past relationships. Then, contemplate and connect with your inner peaceful place where there is no fear. There, you will find the truth; you are significant, special, precious, and worthy of love and respect. You are strong and powerful enough to change your life. With these healings and realizations, you can access your inner strength, conquer your fears, and stand up for yourself to change your life for the better.

Exercise: Standing Up for Yourself

1. Imagine a beautiful sunshine beyond the dark clouds of negative thoughts and emotions in your mind.

2. Say to yourself:
   I am strong, magnificent, and powerful.
   I am invincible.
   I can stand up for myself and change any situation for the better.

3. Ask yourself: What do I want to create in my life instead?

Self-Blaming

Here is the last part of the session with Kristine.

Hiro: Kristine, remember the experience with your brother again and tell him everything you wanted to tell him then. When you're finished telling him everything, take a deep breath, and say, "I forgive you, and I liberate myself from painful emotions." Then, watch him disappear, and say, "I forgive me for putting myself in a victim spot for many years."

Kristine: Yes.

Hiro: How do you feel now?

Kristine: I feel refreshed in my heart. It's like opening a door to a totally new life!

Kristine spoke to Tony that night and broke up with him immediately. A year later, she sent me a message.

"Hello, Hiro! You might have heard about what happened to me already, but I broke up with Tony right after your session. Then, I found another man who treats me very well, and I got married, became the mother of his two little kids, and now, I am pregnant. Thanks for your help!"

While not standing up for yourself can cause you to feel anger toward another person, it can also cause you to feel anger toward yourself; you could blame yourself for not being courageous enough to stand up for yourself. Over time, the energy of anger builds up so much that you can feel the physical sensation of it in your body. This not only becomes the cause of profound stress, but it also takes away your creativity and resourcefulness. To let go of anger, you need to forgive the other person *and* yourself.

Exercise: Forgiving Yourself

1. Think back to a moment when you got angry at yourself.

2. Tell your past self why you were angry with him/her.

3. When you're finished, say, "I forgive you. You might not be perfect, but I love you for who you are."

4. Imagine hugging your past self. Notice how different you feel.

5. Ask yourself: What would I do if I loved myself unconditionally?

One-Sided Giving

One-sided giving is where there is an imbalance of giving and receiving in a relationship. For example, one person may always give, while the other person always receives. The act of giving and receiving includes not only money and material things but also emotional support. A typical situation I observe in one-sided relationships is when one person is always supplying money, daily needs, attention, and love, while the other person shows limited or no respect, appreciation, and attention.

Amanda was a successful businessperson who was doing well financially. When she met Tom, he reminded her of a boy she had a crush on during her school days. Tom was a musician, who dreamed of sharing his passion with the world. He was a nice, good-looking guy who attracted lots of female fans but struggled to become a major player in the music industry.

When Amanda started dating Tom, she knew he did not have much money, so she paid for everything. She loved his music and wanted to support his career, so when he was in need of money for his projects, she was happy to provide financial support. It gave her a sense of satisfaction. Tom was very grateful for her contributions, and their relationship became closer and more intimate. They had beautiful moments together, and she could feel a strong connection with him.

A few years passed, and Tom became a popular musician with a larger fan base and a decent income. Still, he asked for financial support from Amanda, and she responded to his requests. As he became busier and busier, the time the couple spent together decreased, and she had a hard time connecting with him to talk. She was concerned when he stopped responding to her phone calls and texts. When it came to a point where he only contacted her for money, she expressed her concerns and asked him to spend more time with her. He got upset, saying she lacked patience and that he was too busy to spend more time with her. After this argument, he stopped communicating with her completely. Realizing that Tom loved her because of her money, she became devastated and didn't know what she wanted to do anymore. I bet there were several things Amanda needed to learn from this experience, but it's unfortunate that she learned them the hard way.

> **Amanda:** Hiro, I feel so insecure and small, and I feel like I am nothing. Worthless. I know he dated me for money, but I still want him back. He completely ignores me now. I don't know what to do. Please help.

> **Hiro:** That must be very difficult for you, Amanda.

> **Amanda:** Yes...

> **Hiro:** I am sorry you are going through this, but I know you deserve to be loved fully and completely, and I am sure this

experience will lead you to a brighter future. Let's start with how you feel. How would you describe your feelings right now?

Amanda: I am devastated, small, insecure, worthless, and nothing.

Hiro: Where do you feel this in your body?

Amanda: In my heart.

Hiro: If it had a color, what might that be?

Amanda: Dark blue or dark green.

Hiro: OK. Now, I would like you to imagine going deep into that dark blue or green energy in your heart, and find somebody inside. Who do you find?

Amanda: I see myself when I was around twenty years old. She is standing in the dark, alone and sad.

Hiro: What happened?

Amanda: She is missing Mark, my brother who is one year younger than me. We used to be very close, like twins—always doing things together, dancing together, and helping each other. Since our parents were busy and not present in our childhood, we relied on each other. But after he chose to go to a university overseas, we became distant and lost our connection. We had an argument right after he entered the university, and then we stopped communicating completely.

Hiro: She misses him, and it makes her sad?

Amanda: There is more to it. It is like she lost all her energy. She is feeling purposeless and worthless. She used to spend a lot of energy helping him with little things, like homework and his relationships. She defended him when somebody was talking bad about him. He helped her with many things, too. When she got bullied, he fought for her. Now that he is gone, she feels insecure, and she doesn't know what she wants to do.

Hiro: Why is this connection with Mark so important for her?

Amanda: I guess… it gave her energy, motivation, and… meaning. Perhaps, even a sense of purpose. It made her feel strong, important, and significant, when she helped her brother. When he thanked her, she felt proud of herself too.

Hiro: Strong, important, significant, and proud. Do these qualities you possess ever change with or without Mark?

Amanda: No, you're right. They don't change.

Hiro: What might be some ways in which you can experience these qualities in your life today?

Amanda: Let's see… I can experience them when I do something nice and kind for someone, like the act of giving or a good deed.

Hiro: Act of giving. Good deed. Tell me, how does it make you feel when you do that?

Amanda: I feel happy, joy, and proud of myself.

Hiro: What happens if the person who receives your gift does not show gratitude or doesn't give anything back to you in return? How does that make you feel?

Amanda: It doesn't matter. I can still feel happy, joy, and proud of myself. It's like I am happy with becoming a better version of myself when I do a good deed.

Hiro: Very well. Now, imagine yourself around twenty years old again, sad and alone. Imagine coming close to the twenty-year-old you and hugging her. Hold her in your arms. How does she react?

Amanda: I feel her pain is getting healed.

Hiro: Now, say to her, "It's OK. You are safe. I am here for you. I love you. You are not alone anymore. You are strong, important, and significant. And I am proud of you."

Amanda: She is relieved, relaxed, smiling, and almost sleeping in my arms.

Hiro: How do you feel?

Amanda: Oh, I feel better. I feel something heavy in my heart has just been washed away.

If one person is always giving to maintain the relationship, it is a trade, not love. As with Amanda's case, even if the act of giving started out of love, it can turn into a trade-based relationship later on. Love does not have to be unconditional; in partnerships, there are some conditions that should be put in place to maintain close relationships, such as faithfulness, trust, and communication. But if a relationship is based on material possessions or social conditions, such as money, residence, or the quality of living, it does not serve in building a deep connection that satisfies both souls. To cultivate a quality relationship, you need to have understanding, trust, and respect for each other, and you must do things for the other person simply for the joy of giving, rather than being driven by the fear of losing them.

Exercise: Joy of Giving

1. Think of someone in your life you hold dear.

2. Suppose you are given an opportunity to give that person anything you want, no matter the price, but it must be anonymous—what might make them truly happy?

3. Imagine giving the gift to the person anonymously and watching their reaction from a distance. Notice how you feel in your heart.

4. Ask yourself: What can I do today to experience this same feeling?

Self-esteem

In one-sided relationships, self-worth issues are often involved. In these situations, the giver identifies his/her worthiness with something external—like finances, material possessions, or social power. They believe they need to give something to be loved. On the flipside, they believe they are not worthy of love simply for being who they are. Therefore, when the receiver takes it for granted and doesn't show appreciation, it makes the giver feel insecure. As a result, they feel the need to give more so they can continue to be worthy of receiving love.

Let's see what happened with the rest of Amanda's session.

Hiro: Now, I would like you to imagine your brother Mark back when you were around twenty years old. How is he feeling?

Amanda: He is worried about her, my younger self.

Hiro: What does he want to tell you?

Amanda: He says... he loves her as a sister and wants her to be happy.

Hiro: Beautiful. Please ask him if he loves her because she takes care of him?

Amanda: He says no.

Hiro: Then, why does he love her?

Amanda: He loves her because... he just loves her. There is no reason. He loves her just for who she is. It never changes, no matter what happens.

Hiro: Brilliant. Now, bring this message to her—your younger self. How does she react?

Amanda: She is crying, but she is happy... happy crying. It's like a big, icy block in her heart is melting away now.

Hiro: Say to her, "You are worthy of being loved for who you are."

Amanda: She is jumping around!

Hiro: Excellent. Would you like to create a vision for a desirable relationship going forward?

Amanda: Yes

Hiro: Imagine the most desirable relationship you want. What are you noticing?

Amanda: I see myself enjoying the act of giving to my partner and many other people, and I am feeling the joy and gratitude of experiencing a better version of myself. I am not expecting anything in return. But I also see my partner is supporting and helping me a lot, just like Mark did to me.

Hiro: How does this make you feel?

Amanda: I am happy, and I feel intimate, sweet love between us. I feel strong, significant, and important. I am proud of myself. I feel we are growing together and collaborating for the same vision. I feel my life has an important meaning.

Hiro: Very well. Now, you can open your eyes. How do you feel now?

Amanda: I feel so much better and energized. I like the vision I just saw. I understand now that the relationship with Tom was not a healthy one. Does this mean I should just give up on him?

Hiro: It's your choice, Amanda. As you change, your communication to him changes too. He might respond to you differently, or he might not change at all. Then, it is your decision if you would like to fix the relationship with Tom or move on and find somebody else who fits you better. Typically, though, people attract each other because of the lessons they need to learn together. After growing up spiritually like you did today, you and Tom might not make a good match anymore because he still needs to learn his lesson to catch up with you. You can choose to stay with him and help him grow, or you can choose to move on and find another person who fits you better. It's up to you.

Amanda: I don't think I would stick with him. I am ready to create the desirable relationship I want!

What happened after this? Of course, Amanda broke up with Tom, and she met another man and is enjoying the kind of relationship she saw in her vision.

She also reconnected with her brother, Mark, and now, they are talking about their lives and supporting each other like they used to as children.

Giving to others serves you well when you do it from a place of gratitude without expecting anything in return. But if the giving is necessary to maintain your worthiness, your emotions can easily be affected by others, and you will experience an unstable emotional life. The truth is you deserve to be loved for being who you are, and your worthiness will never change, no matter what happens, because it is already within you. You've inherited all the virtuous qualities from God, and they live inside you.

Exercise: Inherited Qualities Inside

1. Imagine a beautiful sunshine beaming beyond the dark clouds of negative thoughts and emotions in your mind.

2. Imagine going inside that sunshine.

3. Ask yourself: What virtuous qualities are present here?

Punishment

When either the giver or the receiver is not satisfied, they often use punishment to control the other person. If the giver is not satisfied with the behavior of the receiver, they may stop giving and demand that the receiver corrects their behavior, so they can feel appreciated, respected, and significant. This makes the relationship worse. The receiver might correct their behavior temporarily but continue to live with a victim mentality. Eventually, anger will start to build up toward the giver, deteriorating the relationship. Also, if the receiver is not satisfied with what they receive from the giver, they may completely stop communicating or stop giving gratitude, respect, and love. This is harsh; the giver will feel like they are losing love. It will make them feel controlled, unworthy of love, and small. Then, the giver will desperately try to fix the situation by giving whatever the other person demands.

In both situations, the quality of the relationship gets worse, putting both parties in a victim mindset. This sort of punishment behavior is observed in different kinds of relationships, such as employer and employee, teacher and student, public figure and fans, server and client, and so on. Has anyone ever completely stopped communicating with you for no apparent reason? It might be that the person is punishing you for what they believe they should have received from you.

When a relationship is controlled by fear, true love cannot be cultivated. You might want to ask yourself if it is worth investing your time and energy to hold on to such a relationship. If you were to fix it, you would first need to address the fear of losing love and the fear of being controlled, then identify your internal worthiness. With this, you will have clarity, peace of mind, and the capacity to connect deeply with the other person. When you attain this peace of mind, you won't feel the need to give to be loved. Then, you can decide if you want to continue the relationship with a different energy or walk away and find somebody else. The choice is yours.

Not Good Enough

Karen was the second daughter to her parents, who always compared her to her elder sister Ellen, the smart, good-looking, and popular one. Their mother always commended Ellen, and said, "Karen, your sister did a lot better than you did at your age. You should be able to do what she did." Karen admired Ellen and tried to do the same as her sister, but no matter how hard she tried, her sister always did things a lot better and attracted a lot of attention from everyone. When Karen decided to work at a local business after high school instead of going to college, her mother supported her decision, but she noticed disappointment on her mother's face and in the tone of her voice. This made her believe she was a disappointment and that she was not good enough.

Meanwhile, Ellen graduated from one of the top universities in the country and started working in investment banking. It was a competitive work environment, but the reward was high. There, she experienced disappointment in herself; there were so many others who were smarter, performed better, and were better looking and more popular. Unfortunately, the salary reflected her performance, and she was impressed by how much money her colleagues made in the same job while she crawled around the base salary range. There was no area where she could be better than her colleagues. She did not know how to handle the situation because this was the first time in her life that she felt inferior to others. She got depressed, and after a while, gave up on herself, and said, "It's just the way it is. I'm not good enough."

Karen, on the other hand, worked so hard to prove herself and become "enough." She did well in her first job, then went into a sales job, where she did very well year after year, making far more money than her elder sister. It made her feel better about herself, and she was proud, but her mother still seemed to favor her sister, continuing to commend her for how good she was. Karen felt frustrated with still being unable to prove herself to her mother and kept working hard. Even though she was a success in her career by anybody's standards, she still felt insignificant and had this urge to work hard every day until she was exhausted. She was still trapped by the feeling of not being good enough and had not gained the peace of mind she was longing for.

When Karen came to me for a private session, she was stressed, exhausted and wanting to create balance in her life.

Hiro: Karen, what would you like to work on today?

Karen: I want to be able to rest. I am a workaholic and cannot allow myself to rest. I am aware of it but still can't rest, and now, I am working to exhaustion.

Hiro: How is this making you feel?

Karen: I feel miserable. I have achieved a lot at work, I am making a lot of money, but I am miserable in my life. I don't know what to do.

Hiro: Miserable. I would like you to imagine going into the feeling of misery, now find somebody inside. Who do you find?

Karen: It's me, around nine years old. She's disappointed and angry.

Hiro: Angry toward whom?

Karen: My mother and elder sister Ellen. Mother always favored Ellen and judged me in comparison to her. Ellen was so good at everything, and I couldn't catch up.

Hiro: Then, what did you do?

Karen: I tried my best to be as good as Ellen, to prove myself to my mother. I wanted her recognition, approval, and love. She never gave them to me. Even if I did something better than Ellen, Mother didn't give me recognition but commended Ellen for something else.

Hiro: How did that make you feel?

Karen: It was awful. I was sad and angry. I resented both of them, but I never gave up. I worked even harder. And today, I am better than her in every aspect, but my mother still favors her and doesn't give me recognition. I felt like I am never enough, no matter what I do.

Hiro: Ask the nine-year-old girl what she wants instead?

Karen: She wants Mother to listen to her, give her recognition, and hug her. That's all she wants.

Hiro: Karen, I need you to give her what she wants. Pretend you are an angel coming to help her. Imagine sitting next to her and hugging her. Say, "It's OK. You are safe. I am here for you, just for you. I love you. You are a good girl, and you are more than enough."

Karen: She is hugging me hard. She needed to hear that. I feel the energy getting lighter.

Do you feel you are good enough? This feeling of "not being good enough" is prevalent in many parts of the society. Many of my female clients shared with me that their parents wanted a boy, and as a result, they were not good enough from the start. Others told me their parents didn't have much money and had a hard time paying for their education, which made them believe they were the cause of their parents' misfortune. Those who had abusive parents believed they deserved punishment because there was something wrong with them. Other causes of "not being good enough" include comparisons to siblings, rejection from a first love, bankruptcy, and other misfortunes.

Do you work yourself to exhaustion? Do you easily give up on yourself? This belief that you're not good enough makes you feel insignificant and insecure, decreases your confidence, and lowers your self-esteem. Every time you experience failure or a less than desirable outcome, you tell yourself you are not good enough. Then, you either keep working hard to become enough or give up on yourself altogether. Every time you don't see the desired outcome, you give up on it, which perpetuates the cycle of not feeling good enough and not being able to achieve your dreams. You get disappointed with things in your life, and say, "It's just the way it is," creating a mental habit of looking for something wrong in yourself instead of appreciating who you are in the present moment.

What caused you to believe you are not good enough? Through my work, I've found that this mindset is typically created in childhood through your interactions with your parents, siblings, relatives, friends, and teachers. Back then, you didn't have the power to discern and decide which ideas to accept or reject, and you learned to evaluate yourself based on external qualities and achievements. There is also an idea of scarcity that comes into play in this. Scarcity refers to the limited resources in our lives. Food is limited, energy is limited, skills and talents are limited, and the love and attention from parents are limited. Because these resources are limited, you receive only what you deserve, and you say, "I don't deserve this because I'm not good enough."

How can you let go of this mindset?

The first step is to understand that the idea of "not being good enough" is an illusion created by fears. Since childhood, you've learned to judge yourself based on conditions set by others—parents, grandparents, siblings, teachers, and so on. These conditions are their opinions; they might say you are good enough one day but change their opinion the next day. Their judgment has nothing to do with the truth about your worthiness. Then, who is the best person to determine if you are good enough? You! You know everything about yourself, and you're the best person to evaluate your worthiness. It doesn't matter what other people say about you; they cannot know more about you than you do.

The second step is to accept that you are already good enough, no matter what happens. As I discussed in the Game of Life Theory, you are a soul who decided to join this game of life. As a soul, you are on your journey to return home to the consciousness from which all souls were born. You've inherited all the highest qualities from the origin, and you are on a journey to remember and embody them. The truth is you have the same worthiness that you had at the point of origin. How can you not be enough? You are good enough and you deserve all the best!

In our human lives, everyone expresses their inherited qualities from the origin in different ways, and they are all good enough in their own ways. Everyone deserves love, joy, and happiness.

With awareness from these two steps, the last step would be to accept yourself fully. You might have had experiences of being judged by others, which caused you pain. Those people might not be the perfect parents, family members, or teachers, but quite frankly, nobody is perfect in this world. Everyone is on a journey to learn lessons through experiences, and we all have our own learning curve. You should not wait for people to become perfect, nor should you depend on their judgment. Instead, you can be the perfect parent, family member, or teacher for yourself. You can identify the part of you that carries the pain, accept yourself for who you are, and love yourself unconditionally. This way, you can be good enough for yourself, no matter what happens in your life.

Here is the rest of Karen's session.

Karen: She is now grown up, around eighteen years old. She is standing tall, proud of herself.

Hiro: Please ask her what would really make her happy.

Karen: She says dancing and singing. Yeah, I used to dance and sing when I was younger, but I stopped at some point.

Hiro: Very well. Now, if you will, promise her you will dance and sing going forward.

Karen: Ok. Yeah, she is happy! She is dancing and singing there.

Hiro: How would you describe this feeling now?

Karen: I feel joy! I feel I can give myself recognition and approval to enjoy life a lot more. I love the idea of being joyful, and I would like to experience more of that. And I know I am more than enough. I don't need my mother to tell me that. I feel lighter on my shoulders, and I feel relaxed.

Hiro: Excellent. Let's take a deep breath, invite the eighteen-year-old girl back into your heart and fill your heart with this joyful energy.

After the session, Karen seemed to have found a new motivation in life to love herself and seek more joy in life. She started going out to dance and sing with her friends, taking more days off from work for trips to wellness retreats, and is now preparing to pursue a wellness business of her own. She told me she found her authenticity, and it is making her happy every day.

Exercise: Allow Yourself to Dream

1. Remember a moment when you were judged by others. Imagine listening to your past self's feelings, thoughts, and emotions.

2. When they're finished, embrace him/her with a hug.

3. Tell her/him:
    It doesn't matter what others told you.
    You are good enough.
    You are loved for who you are.
    You have everything you need within yourself.
    I love you and support you completely, no matter what happens.

4. Notice how your younger self reacts.

5. Ask yourself: If everything in my life exceeds my most optimistic expectations, what will my life be like in five years?

STAGE 2. BEING PRESENT

Henry met Sayuri when she came to the U.S. from Japan to study English. When he got a job offer in New York, he proposed to Sayuri, and she happily accepted. They got married and moved to New York together to start a new life. Henry's new workplace was a very competitive environment, but the pay was good; he was able to afford a nice condo in the center of Manhattan. It took him a lot to catch up with his job expectations, and he was getting overwhelmed day by day, spending most of his time working, even when he was at home. On the other hand, Sayuri wanted to find a job in New York but learned that it took more than a year to get a work permit. She was disappointed and didn't know what to do. She needed somebody to talk to and possibly ask for advice and support.

The couple did the best they could to spend time together, going to restaurants, shopping, and watching movies, but Henry was preoccupied with his work and was not mentally available to listen to her. Over time, Sayuri became lost because she had no one to talk to. She didn't have friends in New York, she wasn't yet comfortable with her English, and she felt alone at home, even when Henry was physically there. She desperately needed someone to talk to, so she found a man on the internet. This man was available to listen to her and was fluent in Japanese. They started communicating frequently on social media, met in person when he traveled to New York, and eventually deepened their relationship.

One day, Sayuri got a phone call as she was writing an email to her internet fling. She left the room to take the call, leaving her computer open. Henry was resting on the sofa, preoccupied with his work, but somehow glanced at her computer and discovered what was going on. He was shocked. When she hung up the call, they got into an argument. He was so angry and blamed her for her infidelity. She admitted what had happened and told him she was not proud of it, but she also confronted him. She told him she desperately needed support from him, but he was not available at all, which left her no choice but to find somebody who was.

After hours of arguments, the two decided to fix their relationship. Henry agreed to give her more attention and love, and Sayuri agreed to terminate her relationship with the man. In the beginning, it seemed like things were working very well, but it was only on the surface. Both of them realized their relationship had already broken into pieces. They wanted to believe anything was possible, so they tried hard to improve the relationship and make a happy family, but it was clear there was no more chemistry. The effort of trying to fix the relationship when there was so much emotional baggage inside was painful for both of them. Two years later, they decided to divorce and move on to different paths.

After a while, Henry started dating another woman. He had a lot of fun with her, and the relationship became serious, but when she expressed a desire for marriage, he stopped seeing her. The thought of marriage triggered emotions from the past, and he couldn't justify getting married again. After a while, he started dating another woman, and the same thing happened. They had a good time together and developed a serious relationship, but the thought of marriage reminded him of the painful experiences in the past, which stopped him completely. He couldn't bear the possibility of going through the same pain again. Both of those women loved him, and they were compatible with him, but he had a strong resistance to the pain he associated with marriage. His mind was trapped by his past emotions, and he could not face the opportunity to happy.

Henry was reluctant when he came to see me. He revealed that someone had encouraged him to visit me.

Hiro: Henry, what would you like to work on today?

Henry: I am afraid of marriage. I want to heal my traumatic memories from my first marriage.

Hiro: What happened?

Henry: She cheated on me. I got mad first, but later, I understood she had a reason to do so. I was not taking care of her at all back then. I felt guilty. We tried to fix it, but it didn't work. The period of trying to fix it was painful, and I just don't want to get married anymore.

Hiro: You don't want marriage, or you don't want the pain?

Henry: Well... I don't want the pain, right.

Hiro: If you remember the pain, where do you feel it in your body?

Henry: In my heart, throat, stomach, and forehead.

Hiro: Which one is the strongest?

Henry: Heart.

Hiro: OK. I would like you to imagine going inside of that painful feeling in your heart. I would like you to find somebody inside.

Henry: I don't see anybody.

Hiro: If there is somebody inside, who might that be?

Henry: Hm, it would be myself when my wife cheated on me.

Hiro: How is he feeling?

Henry: He is angry and sad. He is feeling guilty. He is blaming himself.

Hiro: What else does he want to tell you?

Henry: He says he must be punished. He didn't give attention to his wife and left her alone, pushed her to the edge.

Hiro: What does he need?

Henry: He is looking for forgiveness and love. He feels that he failed.

Hiro: Henry, I need you to do something. Imagine coming closer to yourself back then and hugging him. Say, "It's OK. You are safe. I am here for you. I love you. You are forgiven. Your punishment is over. You can give yourself love, happiness, and joy."

Henry: He is breathing deeper. He is calmer.

Hiro: Ask him what he learned from the experience.

Henry: He learned the importance of caring for others. He learned the need to really listen and understand others.

Hiro: Excellent. Now, tell him, "You learned enough now. Your lesson has been completed. You can care for others, listen, and understand others without needing to have this pain, without needing to punish yourself."

Henry: I feel that he is lighter. He is standing tall.

In life, we all experience challenges or "failures." Each such event causes emotional wounds. Every time you experience a similar situation, you remember the painful emotions, and that drags you down. You lose confidence, suppress your capacity, and lose the opportunities in front of you. However, these challenges in the past are not meant to disempower you; they are meant to teach you something and aid your growth. The painful emotions are a reminder for you to retrieve the lessons and let go of the past, so you can live fully in the present moment.

Every life event happens for a reason. Sometimes they show up to give you a new direction, deliver an important message, connect you with someone, or give you an opportunity to grow. When you're faced with an opportunity to grow, a situation has been prearranged for you to stretch yourself beyond your limit. On the surface, it seems like it's meant to test your physical and mental capacities, but the real ordeal is different: the situation triggers your biggest fear—one you don't dare face—and you get defeated. You give up. But your life never gives up on you; it continues to create the same situation again and again, so you can face the fear head-on. When you finally conquer the fear, you'll have learned precious lessons and can benefit from the rewards that come from the victory.

Here is the rest of Henry's session.

Hiro: Excellent. Would you like to create a vision for a desirable relationship going forward?

Henry: Yes.

Hiro: Imagine the most desirable relationship you want in your life. What do you notice?

Henry: I am caring for my partner. I am looking into her eyes and listening to her well. I am understanding her feelings, and she does the same for me too. She cares for me well. There is a sort of connection between us, a deeper connection than ever before, and I feel peaceful and relaxed.

Hiro: Excellent. What else are you noticing?

Henry: I feel that I am proud of myself for being in this relationship, and I am confident that we can overcome any challenge and grow together. We are happy and joyful. I see a lot of exciting visions for the future.

Hiro: Excellent. Now, silently say to yourself, "This is in my life now."

Henry: Yes.

Hiro: How do you feel now?

Henry: I feel good! I feel like something that was stuck in my heart is gone. I feel my heart is refreshed.

Hiro: How do you feel about marriage now?

Henry: Oh, I feel I can get married again. This is good.

Two months later, Henry became romantically interested in one of his colleagues. When he asked her out, she said, "I will go out with you, but only if you are serious about a committed relationship. I mean, marriage." He was able to say yes from his heart for the first time in a long time. They started dating and got married a year later.

Exercise: Repeating a Challenge

1. Think of a challenge in your life that has repeated over and over.

2. Ask yourself: What is this trying to teach me?

Fear of Failure

What is the one thing that stops people from making their dreams come true? It's the fear of failure. Nobody is exempt from this. Many successful people have struggled with and overcome fear—Oprah Winfrey, Bill Gates, Steven Spielberg, Michael Jordan, J.K. Rowling, and Colonel Sanders, to name a few. It would be nice if everyone reached the destination they sought, but in reality, so many people give up on their dreams or don't even take action because of fears. Let's look at an example.

Akira looked so weak when I met him. He owned a restaurant in a city close to one of the most ancient and important shrines in Japan. He was doing everything by himself in the restaurant—cooking food, serving customers, operating the cash register, buying inventory, cleaning the space, doing the accounting and marketing, and managing the website. He came to me because the restaurant was losing money. It was not getting enough customers to make a profit. He tried various ways to attract customers, but they didn't work as he expected. He believed he could make it work somehow and promised to never give up, but after three years of such continued attempts and failures, he felt helpless and powerless. He ran out of money and had debt from three banks. Worst of all, he was exhausted and just couldn't carry on anymore. That was when he called me.

My big question to him was, "Why are you doing this all by yourself?" He told me he couldn't hire staff because he was running out of money, and he couldn't ask for help from his family members because he had to be strong enough to never let them worry about his business. He had not even told his wife about the situation. His wife was from a wealthy family, and they were happy to support his business, but he needed to prove himself as a man and was never able to ask for money from his in-laws. I was no expert on the restaurant business, but it was clear that some of these beliefs were making his situation worse, and I felt sorry for him for carrying so much burden on his shoulders.

I asked if he loved the work with the restaurant business, and he said no. He loved cooking for his family and friends when he was younger, but it became a job—something he had to do after he was trained to be a chef for a Japanese restaurant. He already lost his passion because of the difficult situation, but he didn't know what else he could do. Besides, he needed to repay the debt. This made me feel sorry for him; how sad it must have been to lose his passion for what he loved in the past. Have you ever experienced something like that before?

Then, I asked him what he wanted to do instead if money was not a problem. He paused for a moment and started talking about his dream. He wanted to be a stand-up comedian. He loved to talk in front of people and make them laugh. He sometimes had the opportunity to do so, and he experienced pure joy and happiness. It was beautiful to watch him talk about his dreams—smiling, shining, and energetic. I was convinced he could make people laugh so much in that state of mind, so I said, "Why don't you follow that dream?"

At first, he was delighted to hear my suggestion, but immediately frowned, and said, "No, I can't. Comedy is a competitive business. I don't think I can make it. And I have to continue this restaurant for my family."

"Do you want to spend the rest of your life like this and give up your dream of becoming a comedian?" I asked.

He was already pushed to the edge because of the situation with his restaurant, and this question was too hard for him. He started crying loudly. "It's impossible for me. I cannot do this any longer. I am going to break apart. And I don't want to give up my dream, and I am so scared of failing again, either with the restaurant or as a comedian."

He had hit rock-bottom. He had lost all his confidence and control. The good thing was he knew what gave him joy, and that was something outside of his existing business. I worked with him on several occasions to lessen his need to be strong, the need to prove himself to his in-laws, and the need to do everything by himself. I also helped him heal his emotional pains from numerous failures, increase his confidence, and create a future vision to regularly perform as a comedian and experience joy in life.

After releasing the beliefs of pain and fear, he became more hopeful, flexible, and open. Then, finally, he spoke to his wife about the situation, asked for financial support, and started taking action to resolve the situation with the restaurant and making progress on his dream of becoming a comedian. The dream gave him hope, and the hope gave him the energy to transform his life. It was beautiful watching him flourish.

Have you ever experienced a rock-bottom moment? Akira's situation might be an extreme case, but so many people are going through challenges that push them to the edge, causing them to get overwhelmed and give up on their dreams. When they come to me for help, they always talk about the problems with the status quo, then talk about their dreams like they're somewhere far beyond the sky. It often seems to me that they were putting themselves in the wrong fight. The status quo was a distraction so they wouldn't have to face their fear of failure.

I have put myself in wrong fights many times in my life, and I know how difficult it is to realize that because, for me, a problem often seems more important than my future vision. Years ago, I decided to change my career to spiritual healing and life coaching, but I overwhelmed myself with the daily issues and problems at my corporate job, and avoided acting on my vision for many months. At another time, I wanted to move to another country to venture into new opportunities, but I kept adding local projects onto my calendar many months ahead, saying "Well, I hope to move to another country someday, but not yet, not now." I was in an illusion that I had no time and resources to proceed with my vision, but in reality, I was sabotaging myself by putting myself into that illusion. What helped me wake up and get out of the illusion was this question: "Am I doing this to avoid my vision?

How about you? Are you in a wrong fight right now? What might you be avoiding?

Exercise: *What might you be avoiding?*

1. Think about the activities you spend a lot of time doing every day.

2. Ask yourself: What might I be avoiding that is more important than this?

There Is No Failure

Throughout childhood, we all learn to judge ourselves. Did I do it right or wrong? Am I a good or bad person? Did I win or lose? Our self-esteem fluctuates depending on our judgment and the judgment from others, and over time, we all aim to be successful in life—becoming an important person, acquiring fame, winning a big competition, making a fortune, and so on. These judgments are based on the results of our goals, and no matter how well we do in the process of reaching said goals, if we judge it as a failure, the experience becomes a bitter memory. You might get angry, sad, or disappointed.

However, from the perspective of the Game of Life, the outcome is not as important as the process of getting there. If you consider that the real purpose is to grow through experiences, then the definitions of "success" and "failure" become somewhat different. Success in the Game of Life is about how much you grow in the process and what you experience in the physical reality. It does not matter whether you meet the expectations of an activity.

If you experienced something and it contributed to your growth, it was a success. In that sense, there is no failure in your life because every experience presents an opportunity to grow in some way. If you experience a dull moment, you learn how it feels to live in a dull moment, and you can avoid it in the future. If you get angry at yourself, you learn how it feels to be angry, and you understand what you want instead. It might be counterintuitive, but these are still valuable experiences and lessons from the perspective of the Game of Life.

One of the drawbacks of the traditional ideas of "success" and "failure" is that we look for joy and fulfillment at the end, and push ourselves to work hard during the process to get to it. However, if the purpose is growth, you can experience joy and fulfillment every step of the way instead of waiting until the end. When you are focused on enjoying the present moment, your activity is no longer work, but rather, it becomes the act of joy and fulfillment.

Exercise: No Failure

1. Think about an experience in your life that you'd regard as a "failure."

2. Ask yourself: How did I grow from that experience?

Taking Action

Even when I knew what I wanted in my heart, there were times when I didn't take action, and postponed my dreams. Sometimes it seemed like the right time to take chances, but I was afraid of failure and came up with all kinds of excuses. "It's not the right time. I am too busy now. I am not well prepared. There will be a better time in the future." Have you ever had such excuses in your mind? Sure, there will continue to be opportunities in the future, but they will be different ones. The same opportunity will never come again, and

I was missing important opportunities every time I decided to not take a chance. As Wayne Gretzky famously said, "You miss 100% of the shots you don't take."

You might say you cannot risk your family's safety and well-being, but I would say that's also an excuse. You just need to figure a way to not put your family at risk. Besides, do you want your kids to remember you as someone who gave up on your dreams because of them? Kids learn from how we live our lives. They might end up making the same mistakes you did.

It is easy to avoid taking action and to stay in your comfort zone pretending everything is fine, but does that environment help you grow? It does not push you, and it certainly does not give you excitement. Unfortunately, many people spend their whole life like this. According to a survey conducted with people in their 80s, when asked about regrets in life, many of them responded by saying, "I wish I had had more adventures." They had been trapped in their fears and couldn't get out of their comfort zone. Yes, it might give you a peaceful life, but tell me, without freedom from fear, how can you experience real joy and fulfillment?

The chance you have in front of you is the precious opportunity to conquer your fears and go into an exciting adventure. If there was a chance you could liberate yourself from fears and experience freedom, would you take it? The adventurous road is not a paved road. It pushes you beyond your comfort zone and tests your strength, patience, perseverance, courage, and faith. But you will feel more alive and authentic than you would living the rest of your life contained in a small cage. You will discover how unique you are, why you came to this game of life, and what can truly give you joy and fulfillment in life.

If you there's something you want in your heart, take a chance and jump! There will be no guarantees, and there will be a lot of uncertainties. But when you are walking on a path toward your dream, every step you take will give you joy or teach you a valuable lesson. You won't work for money or survival anymore; you'll work for joy. You are the creator of your life, and you can make yourself fully alive. By following your heart, you will be guided to activate your highest qualities and talents and fulfill your life missions.

Exercise: Taking Action

1. Think about something you want to do but keep postponing.

2. Ask yourself: Which is worse, failing or never trying?

Ebb and Flow of Life

Back in 2003, I joined a company as a project manager. The company's business was rapidly growing, and so was the organization. I remember feeling a huge momentum within the company—although slightly chaotic—because it was growing so fast. The first three years were exciting and expansive, full of learning opportunities and joy. But things started to change during the fourth year, when the company decided to establish more control in the decision-making process. And, at the same time, the market was going into a downturn. It was the time when we started to see the early signs of abnormal trends in the market that later triggered the big financial crisis in 2008, which severely affected the company. As the business slowed down, management decided to downsize the organization, and my team was disassembled. That was shocking and disappointing to me. I was transferred to another department, and was lucky to have very nice colleagues there, but I still felt my time was reaching its end in the company.

At the same time, I was seeing a big momentum shift in something else. I was learning a meditative healing technique as a hobby, and was surprised to experience so much joy and happiness as I practiced it. It was the experience of making a positive difference in somebody else's life that gave me a fantastic feeling. I was amazed to see how the healing technique was spreading so fast to many people through word of mouth. Feeling the momentum and trusting my intuition, I quit the company, and started my own meditation and emotional healing company. My business grew steadily, and eventually, my role started to expand; I was asked by the founder of the healing method to oversee all Japan operations of the meditative healing technique. In the beginning, the healing business was very small, but it was about to catch a growing momentum. In four years, we increased the team of healing instructors from four to more than one thousand!

However, everything has its own natural cycle of growing momentum and shrinking momentum, just like the rise and fall of the waves in the ocean. A few years after we hit one thousand instructors, there was a downturn. The average number of students for healing classes started decreasing. It became harder for instructors to stay profitable, and some of them decided to leave the business. We did various marketing efforts to bring back the momentum, a lot more efforts than we had ever done before, but the results were a lot smaller than what we wished for. One day, I felt like I was walking in a river, going against the current, as if all my efforts were offset by it. I realized it is not wise to resist the momentum. I decided to go with the flow and focus on what I could do, which was providing the best healing service I could for the people who were coming, no matter how small the group.

After a couple of years, this "wintertime" was complete. We didn't do anything different in our marketing efforts, but we started to see more people coming to our healing classes. Interestingly, those people were a new type of audience. They were faster learners who were good at applying the techniques in their lives in practical ways, and they easily became good friends to each other.

According to the Law of Attraction, you attract energies that match your own. But your attraction is also affected by broader energy flows in the universe, such as the momentum of the stars, nature, society, and business. When such momentum is in the rising motion, it is easier to make things happen and create the outcome you want. It's like doing ten things and getting twenty rewards. When the momentum takes a downturn, however, you may do ten things and get only a few rewards. Therefore, to manifest your dream, it is important to keep up with the momentum you are in.

Both in my corporate job and healing business, I experienced a rise and fall in momentum. I learned that the momentum largely influences our activities and outcomes, in addition to our individual efforts, qualities, and intentions. The big question is how can we find the right activity, timing, and momentum? It would be nice if you could read or feel the momentum accurately, but what if you couldn't?

The answer is simple. Seek your life mission. You, as a soul, planned major life events and meetings in your life to guide yourself to the best time to enter your life mission. Prepare yourself through lessons that come your way and be awakened to your life mission at the divine time in your life. This way, you can experience the greatest joy and fulfillment in life.

Exercise: Ebb and Flow of Life

1. Think back to a time when you felt a growing momentum in your work or private life. Feel it swell in your heart.

2. Ask yourself: Where do I find this feeling in my life today?

Shame, Regret, and Guilt

When David was in his early twenties, he met Sasha, a lady from eastern Europe, on a pen pal matching website. After exchanging emails for months, the two decided to meet in her city. They spent the entire first day and night together talking. Then, she took him to some tourist attractions, introduced him to her friends and family, and had an overall good time with him. When he met her brothers and cousins, they asked him to treat Sasha well, and he promised to do so. Coming back home, David started to get worried. He felt like her family members were already accepting him as a possible marriage partner for Sasha, which was very nice and heartwarming, however, he felt the impact of their major cultural differences and didn't feel he could live up to their expectations. He couldn't imagine himself living in her city, and he couldn't imagine her living in his city, either. He decided he should leave her.

Sasha didn't know what was going on with him and continued emailing him as usual. He opened her email but didn't know what to tell her. Before he was able to be brave enough to share his feelings, he received more emails from Sasha, who was starting to worry. He didn't know how to explain what was going on with him, and with time, it became even harder for him to respond. The situation continued for weeks and months, and finally, Sasha gave up and stopped writing him. David felt sorry about all that happened and blamed himself. He was ashamed for not having the courage to share his feelings, and he regretted not writing back to her, ultimately feeling guilty for hurting her feelings.

David was one of my healing colleagues, and he asked me for help because he kept avoiding the issue. His subconscious didn't want to feel the pain again.

Hiro: Tell me, David, how do you feel about what happened?

David: I feel guilty. I want to apologize to her, but it was years ago and we've lost contact already. I cannot resolve it.

Hiro: Imagine looking inside of that guilty feeling. Who do you see?

David: Her. Sasha. She's angry and sad. Helpless.

Hiro: Do you also see yourself near her?

David: Yes. He is small, turning his back, and looking down. Sad and guilty.

Hiro: What does he want to tell you?

David: He says he is coward, not acceptable as a man. He should disappear. He must be punished.

Hiro: OK. David, I need you to do something. Imagine sitting next to him and hugging him. Say, "It's OK. You are safe. I am here for you. I love you. You can learn from this and move on. You can be forgiven."

David: He is looking at me and saying, "Really?" He is not sure about it.

Hiro: Good. Now, imagine him standing with Sasha face-to-face. Let her tell him everything she wants to tell him. Let me know when she finishes.

David: OK... yes, she finished. She expressed anger for a while, but now she is crying.

Hiro: Have him say everything he wants to tell her. Let me know when he finishes.

David: He said, "I apologize. I was wrong. I didn't know what to do."

Hiro: Let him say, "Please forgive me."

David: She said, "I forgive you." And she disappeared.

Hiro: What did you learn from this experience with her?

David: I learned the importance of facing a challenge head-on. I learned to acknowledge my weakness and work to improve it.

Hiro: Good. Now, say to yourself, "I forgive myself and liberate myself from guilt."

David: Yes.

Hiro: Now, how is your younger self?

David: He is breathing deeply. He is relieved. Lighter. He can move on.

Hiro: Very well. How do you feel?

David: I feel a lot better, thank you. But in real life, I lost her contact and cannot say anything to her. What should I do?

Hiro: When you remember what happened, do the same visualization again. When your energy changes, your reality will start changing, too. Let's see what might happen.

David: OK.

Some time later, he received an email from Sasha. She expressed how she felt back when their communication stopped and told him he should never do that to anybody else. David wrote back and apologized for what happened. He knew he was wrong, and when he asked her to forgive him, she replied that she had already forgiven him. She had found another man and was so happy. She wanted him to be happy, too.

Many of us have experiences we are not proud of. Perhaps you betrayed somebody, broke a promise, cheated on your partner, bullied a classmate, physically or emotionally hurt someone, caused someone to suffer because of your decisions, ignored someone who needed help, treated someone unfairly, left your family for your ambition, or disrespected, insulted, or offended somebody. Maybe you allowed yourself to become an alcoholic or drug addict, or perhaps you've committed a crime and victimized somebody. These experiences cause pain in your heart that comes up in your life as shame, regret, and guilt.

Perhaps you thought it was the right thing to do at that moment, but later, you realized it was wrong, and those feelings of shame, regret, and guilt grew bigger inside you. You don't know what to do with them because you cannot go back to the moment and change what happened. You don't dare meet the other person and apologize. Instead, you decide to change yourself and become a better person, pretending nothing happened. However, those feelings do not go away.

Whatever happened took place for a reason. We are all learning from experiences in this game of life, and sometimes we do stupid things or things we are not proud of. It is a part of being a human. We experience the consequences, learn from them, become a better person, and move on. If you learned everything you were supposed to from the experience, you wouldn't have those feelings of shame, regret, and guilt. The fact that you are keeping those feelings within you means you still have something to learn from them.

Those feelings of shame, regret, and guilt hamper your further growth. If you do not resolve them, they will continue to build up and will eventually negatively impact your health. It can also be excruciating if your past actions and behaviors directly went against your core values and who you're striving to become. Those feelings contain a lot of dark energies, and they attract the same energy into your life again and again. When a similar situation happens, you might not do the same things, but it will remind you of those difficult feelings. You cannot forget them. You need to give yourself an opportunity to complete the lessons, forgive yourself, and let go.

In addition to accepting the consequences from your past actions and doing all you can to remedy the situation, the most important thing to do is forgive yourself. It would be great if the other person forgave you, but you do not have control over that. You must forgive yourself regardless. You must liberate yourself from the prison of shame, regret, and guilt.

From the perspective of the soul, the past event happened for all parties to grow, which means the other parties have something to learn from the event too. I guarantee when all parties complete their lessons, all hard feelings will disappear and only love will remain. But you cannot force it to happen; you cannot learn something on another's behalf, and you are not responsible for it either. You are only responsible for accepting your consequences, learning from what happened, and moving on. If you wish, you can share the lessons with others so the same thing does not happen in their lives.

Exercise: Shame, Regret, and Guilt

1. Remember a moment when you felt shame, regret, or guilt.

2. Imagine standing in front of the person who was involved in the incident, and saying, "Forgive me."

3. After the person disappears, say, "I forgive myself and liberate myself from this shame (or regret/guilt)."

4. Ask yourself: What might be possible now that I am free from shame (or regret/guilt)?

Extreme Cases

Perhaps you were involved in severe or extreme cases, such as emotional bursts that led to harming others, car accidents that ended up killing someone, or ego-centric behaviors that victimized many others. You might be telling yourself that you will never be forgiven, must be punished forever, and should

go to Hell. Don't believe those things. Of course, you must accept the consequences and fulfill the responsibility that comes with them. But consider
the possibility that it was still part of a life lesson for you to grow. When the
incident happened, you were trapped by your emotions and fear, or perhaps
had been controlled by false beliefs. But that was not the true nature of your
soul. Behind all those emotions, fears, and beliefs, you have higher qualities
within you.

Sometimes a soul chooses to learn a virtuous quality the hard way—
going through the lack of at particular quality to eventually recognize its
importance. For example, if you went through the illusion of "satisfying your
ego at the expense of others" and realized it did not really make you happy,
it might help you recognize the importance of virtuous qualities, like respect,
understanding, gratitude, kindness, and harmony.

You might have taken the most extreme, darkest path to learn something of the opposite extreme. What might that be? As a soul, you wanted to
take a risk and experience that particular quality; therefore, it must be something very precious that is not easy to learn in other ways. It is your responsibility to identify such precious lessons, and if you share the lesson with
others and prevent the same unfortunate things from happening to them,
your experience will serve others well.

Let me tell you this: No matter what happened in the past, it does
not mean you have to suffer in Hell; it does not mean you are undeserving
of God's love; it does not make you a bad soul; it does not make your soul
inferior to the souls of others; and it does not take away your inherent gifts
and virtuous qualities. It is never too late to learn from past mistakes. Accept
the consequences and forgive yourself. Do the best you can to remedy the
situation, and give yourself an opportunity for redemption. It doesn't matter
whether you receive forgiveness from others or not; what matters is how you
grow and who you become. Have a clear vision of who you want to become
and how you want to contribute to the world. Never give up on yourself,

never give up on your life, and continue to aim for the highest version of yourself. After all, this is a game of life for our souls to grow.

Exercise: Extreme Cases

1. Remember the moment when you were involved in an extreme case.

2. Imagine who you were back then.

3. Say to yourself, "I know I've made mistakes. I accept the consequences, and I am committed to fulfilling the responsibility that came with them. I still love myself unconditionally and forgive myself. I allow myself to keep growing and aim for the highest version of myself."

4. Ask yourself: What did I learn from this?

Loss of a Loved One

Several years ago, my friend Sarah met a man named Martin. She had long been waiting to meet her soul mate, the love of her life, and they both believed they were that person for each other. I had the privilege of working with the couple during a conference, and I felt they were actually soul mates. I felt so happy just watching them smile, giggle, and look at each other with those warm, trusting, peaceful eyes. It was as if the whole space around them was shining and sparkling, making others feel happier too. They shared the same values and visions, and I could see they had a deep understanding and respect for each other.

At the time, Martin's job was flexible, so he was able to support Sarah with her coaching and teaching activities as an administrator. Martin helped my whole team too as a salesman, talking to people in the conference and bringing them to our booth so they could experience healing and coaching. He was such a kind, supportive, joyful person; no one could resist listening to him.

A few years later, I heard Martin was going through a serious sickness, and Sarah was accompanying him to the hospital every day. Many of us prayed for him for weeks, but unfortunately, he didn't recover; he moved on to the other side. It was difficult for me to accept why a good man like him had to die so young. I couldn't imagine how difficult it was for Sarah to accept having her soul mate leave her life. When I contacted her, she said, "Hiro, I'm sad, but I'm OK. I am hanging in there somehow. I just don't have the energy or the motivation to do anything now." She stopped all her professional activities and disappeared from any social connections for a while. It took more than a year for her to heal her heart and come back to see us again.

I didn't have the opportunity to give her a healing session, but I met her at another conference. She was as energized and happy as she used to be, and was hopeful and had a future vision. I was so glad to see that she had moved on, and I bet Martin was watching over her from the other side, just like he used to when he was alive.

Have you ever lost a loved one in your life, someone you love the most, the one person you connected with deeply from your heart, the person no one else can replace? People die every day somewhere in the world, and it's a natural transition back to where their soul came from, but still, the loss of a loved one has a profound emotional impact on us. It rips our heart apart, leaving an empty space. You might have lost someone to natural causes, a sickness, accident, suicide, or homicide. You might have lost a new life through miscarriage or abortion. Losing your loved one causes long-standing sorrow, a deep current of sadness that seems to last forever. Many of us don't know how to deal with it and end up getting lost.

You can force yourself to go to work, continue routines like "business as usual," and it helps distract your mind, keeping you from facing the difficult emotions. However, as with other cases we discussed earlier, this deep sadness is stuck in your body and does not leave you automatically, no matter how hard you try to ignore it. The painful feeling keeps reminding you of itself by attracting that same energy in your life, sometimes affecting your health. That sad energy in your body needs to be expressed somehow so that it can get out of your body.

From the perspective of the Game of Life, death is a graduation. It is a liberation from a physical experience and an opportunity for celebration. People do not die accidentally. Even if it happened accidentally from our perspective, there are a lot of things going on behind the scenes at different levels of consciousness. When people die, it is their soul's decision to leave this life at that particular time, date, place, and under that circumstance. It means the life served its soul's purpose well and/or it does not need to serve its purpose any longer.

Sometimes the death of a person has a more profound meaning that triggers precious lessons for the people around that person to learn. The decision of death is made by the soul of the person with prior consultation of all other souls involved. If a father died of sickness in front of the entire family, it means that's how all the souls involved agreed for it to happen. The same applies to any other deaths, be it natural, accidental, a suicide, homicide, miscarriage, or abortion.

Once people pass on to the other side, they feel happy and liberated! They do not want anyone to feel sad or guilty about their death; they want us to be happy and continue with our life journeys. They are hoping everyone can learn something from their death and remember the good memories with them. If you lost your significant other, please know he or she would not expect you to spend the rest of your life alone. They want you to move on and find somebody else who can make you happy. It does not make him/her angry or jealous. Once they pass on to the other side, they are less influenced by their ego, and they purely wish for your happiness.

By the way, just because they moved on to the other side does not mean they left you. They are still with you, but they just don't have a body. As a metaphor, imagine a baseball game. There are eighteen players on the field at once during a baseball game. When one of the players replaces another, the player goes back to the bench and no longer participates in the game, but they're still watching with enthusiasm, cheerleading, giving advice, and enjoying the game alongside the active players. Those people who ended their Game of Life are still watching your game, cheering you on, teasing you, giving you advice, and so on. They are with you more than you can imagine! And when you end your life, they are the first ones to greet you on the other side, and you will have plenty of time to catch up and share a lot of beautiful experiences together.

To heal the pain from the loss of loved ones, you need to let go of the sorrow in your body, which is typically held in your lungs. The energy of sorrow needs to be expressed somehow. The easiest way to do this is to cry. Crying is healing, and it helps release the energy. Find some movies that resonate with your feelings, and let the energy go by crying. Another way to express the energy is through the tone of voice. Find some songs that resonate with your feelings, and let your pain go through the tone of your voice.

Alternatively, visualization helps in healing the pain as well. Imagine yourself as a separate entity that is crying inside the energy of sorrow. In your imagination, hug yourself and say, "It's OK. You are safe. I am here for you. I love you. You are not alone. We can find happiness together."

Exercise: Loss of a Loved One

1. Imagine yourself crying inside the energy of sorrow from the loss of a loved one.

2. Imagine your loved one sitting next to you, hugging you, and saying, "It's OK. You are safe. I am here for you. I love you. You are not alone."

3. Ask yourself: "How does he/she want me to live my life?"

Unborn Baby

Laura was suffering from guilt and sorrow, and asked me for healing.

Hiro: What happened?

Laura: I had a miscarriage. Twice. I am so sad the babies were not able to be born. There must be something wrong with my body or maybe I did something wrong during my pregnancy, and I feel guilty.

Hiro: That must be difficult.

Laura: Yes.

Hiro: OK. Let's do some healings. Where do you feel the feeling of guilt in your body?

Laura: In my heart.

Hiro: I would like you to imagine going inside the energy of that feeling.

Laura: Yes.

Hiro: Who do you see inside?

Laura: I see the babies and me.

Hiro: How are the babies?

Laura: They are smiling and giggling. They are cute!

Hiro: How is 'Laura' doing inside that energy?

Laura: She is sitting on her knees and sobbing.

Hiro: What does she tell you?

Laura: She says… I did wrong. I am a mistake. I am a failure. I am responsible for the miscarriage. I don't deserve to be loved by the babies. I must live in darkness.

Hiro: I see. Now, pretend you are an angel who came to rescue her today. Imagine yourself sitting next to her and giving her a warm hug.

Laura: Yes… she is crying on my chest.

Hiro: Say, "It's OK. You are safe. I am here for you. I love you. You are not a mistake. You deserve to be loved. You deserve happiness."

Laura: She is like, "Really?" She wants to believe it, but she is not sure.

Hiro: Good. Now, let's talk to the babies. Which one do you want to talk to, or would you like to speak to both at the same time?

Laura: I feel I can talk to them at the same time.

Hiro: Good. Then say, "How are you?"

Laura: They're happy!

Hiro: Then say, "What happened with your birthing process?"

Laura: Yes… They say there was something unexpected that did not allow them to live longer.

Hiro: Because of 'Laura'?

Laura: No. They say it was due to some technical issues she did not have control over.

Hiro: How do they feel about her?

Laura: They love her so much and are very grateful for the fact that she gave them a physical life, even if it was for a short period of time.

Hiro: But they were not born alive, right?

Laura: Right. But they had a physical life inside of her body for a while. That gave them the precious experience of being in a physical body. They enjoyed her energy and the experience with her in the physical world.

Hiro: Very well. Now, how is she reacting to this?

Laura: She is relieved and at peace. She is not crying anymore.

Hiro: Good. Now, let the babies come to her and hug her.

Laura: Oh my god, this is beautiful. I am crying.

Hiro: Now, please ask the babies, "Will you try coming to a human life again?"

Laura: They say yes! They say, "Of course. We will do whatever we can to be in her life, whether it is as her children, adopted children, nephew/niece, grandkids, or whatever relationship it can be."

Hiro: Laura, what did you learn from this experience of miscarriage?

Laura: I learned to take care of my body. And I learned to be stronger, hopeful and patient.

Hiro: Can I honor you for caring for your body, your strength, hopefulness, and patience, so you can always demonstrate these qualities without needing to go through pain?

Laura: Yes!

Hiro: How do you feel now?

Laura: I feel so relaxed and safe. I feel positive. I think I can move on.

I met Laura again the following year. She got pregnant again, and she looked so happy! I am sure she will have a happy time having a baby and spending her life as a mother.

I've met many people who have had miscarriages, and I learned that the majority of them suffer from guilt and sorrow. I always tell them their baby will come into their lives again somehow. Birth is a delicate process, and sometimes it does not go as anticipated, even from the perspective of your soul. Even if a baby cannot complete the birthing process to the end, they are still grateful for the experience of having a physical presence. Even if it was only for a short period of time, the time they spent with the mother is precious, special, and an important experience for the baby's spirit.

If the miscarriage was not the soul's plan and the baby was supposed to live a longer human life, they will keep coming back to you at the next possible opportunity, no matter how many attempts it takes. If becoming your child becomes difficult, the spirit will seek alternatives, such as coming to you as an adopted child, a nephew/niece, a grandchild, and so on.

To overcome this, heal the sorrow and guilt, and let them go. Trust that your baby will come into your life someday—one way or another.

Exercise: Unborn Baby

1. Imagine hugging your unborn baby who is smiling and giggling.

2. Ask yourself: If the baby was with me now, how would she/he want me to feel?

Lost Glory

When Ken came to me for a private session, he looked so tired, and I remember wondering what it was that was making him look that way. He didn't look me in the eyes, and he seemed nervous and insecure. He told me he wanted to be "enlightened," and he had hundreds of questions about what enlightenment was and how to get there. To be honest, I was no expert on that subject, but I sat down with him, and asked him what was going on in his life.

He said he was engaged in the transportation business and was making a good living, but he did not have passion for the business and wanted a breakthrough in life. His previous business, an internet-based dating service, was the cause of his current lack of passion. The business was very successful, and it had made him a large amount of money over the years. He enjoyed the fame, social respect, and the high quality of living that the business gave him. He made friends with famous business leaders, celebrities, athletes, etc. When he talked about his experiences during that time, I could see how proud he was of his past. His face lit up, and he spoke with more energy and warmth.

He continued explaining how the situation changed dramatically, how the market had changed and his audience had started looking for something different, something more technologically advanced and convenient, which his business could not keep up with. His sales sharply declined, and he ended up needing to shut down the business. He was devastated and spent some years doing nothing, living off his savings. Eventually, he ran out of savings and started working for a transportation company to support his living. The new job was good—it provided a decent income and a good working environment—but he was not happy there. He was still attached to the previous business, and couldn't help but compare his two drastically different circumstances.

Ken was experiencing the lost glory and was living in the past, unable to focus in the present moment. When I asked him if he wanted to start a new business and make it as successful as his last one, he said, "Yes, but I want to be enlightened before doing a new business. I want to be able to foresee everything that happens in the market so I can win all competitions." What would your reaction be if you heard someone say this? I remember I had a lot of reservations when he told me all of this. Now, I know why. Here are a few reasons his plan of "enlightenment" would go wrong.

Firstly, he was on a quest for significance that would never be satisfied. It is a quest to be greater as much as possible in comparison to others. When you are driven by desire for significance, you want to be more valuable, be more important, have more money, become more famous, and acquire higher social status. The desire makes you believe that you are not significant enough even when you are more than enough already. To increase his worthiness and experience a sense of significance, Ken was looking to external things, like success, fame, social respect, and money. But this is a never-ending quest. No matter how much he succeeded, there would always be somebody else who was better, who had more. His thirst for significance would never be fulfilled, and he would never experience peace of mind. Instead, Ken should've identified his worthiness through his internal qualities, so that he could find peace.

Secondly, his motivation for "enlightenment" was coming from a place of fear, which would stop his spiritual growth and guarantee he would never become truly enlightened. He wanted to gain the ability to foresee the future so he would never lose competitions because he was afraid of failing again. I actually didn't know what exactly he meant when he said "enlightenment." However, assuming it was about a highly evolved state in spiritual development, it's safe to say he would never reach it with fear-based motivation because spiritual development is all about conquering fears and focusing on love. And quite frankly, if he did reach an enlightened state, I guarantee he would no longer be interested in winning competitions or in acquiring fame. For a highly evolved, spiritual person, a business is a vehicle to spread love and peace in the world, not to build wealth for oneself.

Thirdly, his vision was limited by his painful past, a lost glory associated to his previous business. His condition for success was based on his comparison to a past experience; he had to be more "successful" than before to be happy. But the market has changed; whatever he does going forward would be something new, something incomparable to the past.

This attachment to the lost glory can happen to anyone. The glorious days or happy memories of the past can keep your mind stuck there, not allowing you to live in the present moment. I know some business owners who are too attached to their previously successful business systems and try to make it work again and again. Even when the market changes dramatically and the old system clearly no longer works, they do not accept that. The glorious past has made them blind and limited.

There are movie stars, professional athletes, and musicians who have achieved a high level success and later went through a sharp decline, but were so attached to the glorious days of the past that they struggled to adapt to a new identity in the present moment. Attachment to lost glory causes challenges in relationships too. Some people allow themselves to be trapped in a miserable relationship, hoping the sweet, beautiful days will come back. This does not allow them to see the need to face the situation today.

I've had this challenge too. After quitting my corporate job and starting my meditative healing business, I always compared my new business to what I was used to in the previous career, particularly the amount of money involved in my projects. But I realized the value of my current business couldn't be measured solely by my bank account, and I needed to let go of the value system from my previous career. I had to redefine how I evaluated my business and what it meant to be successful.

From the perspective of the Game of Life, the loss of glory is an aspect of universal rhythm, a momentum that is prevalent in everything in our lives. Everything in the universe is vibrating at a unique rhythm. It is a part of the ebbs and flows of life, which you can see in the activities of atoms, the movement of planets, the four seasons, the moon cycle, day and night cycles, and so on. Likewise, each of our lives has a rhythm too. There are times when the energy is going up and everything goes well, and there are times the energy is calming down and everything becomes dormant. If something in your life is slowing down, it is likely that the natural cycle is reaching a completion. It is a time to appreciate all the experiences and lessons, recharge yourself, and prepare for the next cycle.

Many of us, including myself, are tempted to quickly begin a new cycle; however, we cannot force the new cycle to begin immediately, just like we cannot force a seed to sprout during winter. We cannot expect the new cycle, journey, or adventure to be the same as the previous one because the Game of Life cycle is not a circle but rather, an upward spiral. Even if you engage in the same activities, they will be upscaled in some way. New cycles in the Game of Life are typically greater in scale, broader in reach, more virtuous in intention and purpose, and more rewarding for your spiritual growth, thereby giving you more joy and fulfillment. And, of course, you can improve the quality of your life and relationships along the way, if you wish.

If you keep your attachment to the past glory, which is the previous cycle of your rhythm of life, you are sabotaging your own evolution. You need to let go of the past so you can move on to the next chapter of your life. By letting go of the past, you can liberate yourself and experience a new adventure!

To let go of the past and live fully in the present moment, you first need to heal that pain. It is similar to the pain from the loss of loved ones because we all love the good memories and successes of the past; to many of us, it is like losing a child. Perhaps this pain is much less intense than the pain from the loss of loved ones, but it's still powerful enough to make your life miserable if you allow it to.

What happened to Ken afterward? He went through a very difficult, emotional challenge, his Dark Night of the Soul. He struggled but somehow reached a realization that God exists in everyone and everything, which led him to accept himself for who he was without needing to achieve anything. He didn't start a new business, but he found peace and happiness in his life. Is this what it means to be "enlightened?" I don't know. But I do know he made a significant spiritual progress that his soul would be proud of.

Exercise: Lost Glory

1. What glorious moments from your past are you holding on to right now?

2. Look at yourself in the mirror, and say, "It's OK. You are safe. I am here for you, and I love you. You've outgrown your past and are opening to the new."

3. Ask yourself: What might become possible if I make the most adventurous move today?

STAGE 3. SOCIAL ACCEPTANCE

Have you ever wanted to do something that went against common sense? That urge can trigger a fear of social rejection and force you to give up on your dreams.

Back in 2006, I realized I was not happy in my heart even though I achieved all the necessary conditions for happiness. As a result, I started searching for what I wanted in my life. Among the many new things I tried, it turned out to be emotional healing that gave me very special feelings. When people asked me for help with their life challenges, I immediately felt my heart open wide, and I had a genuine desire to alleviate that person's suffering. When I somehow was able to help the person heal their emotional wounds and feel better, I felt so much warmth, peace, love, and magnificence in my heart; it was as if I was able to experience the best version of myself. It was a feeling of being fully alive! Soon, word of mouth spread, and one after another, people started asking me for healing sessions. I really loved doing that work, and I was convinced it was the way I could make myself truly happy. I wanted to experience those feelings every day for the rest of my life, and it didn't take long for me to decide to facilitate emotional healing full-time.

However, it took me several months before I actually made the change. The decision was already made in my heart, but there were many voices in my mind that told me all the negative ideas about healing, which caused an inner conflict.

"Healing is just a hobby! You should stick with your current job."

"Healing can't help you make money and support your living."

"You are too old to start something completely new."

"Women are more capable of healing than men. You are not qualified to do healing."

"Healing is fishy! It is not supported by science."

"People don't pay for healing service."

"People don't understand healing, and they will ignore you."

"People will leave you, and you will be alone."

These voices were the beliefs of the society I belonged to, and they were toxic enough to disempower my passion for healing. I started to feel like healing wouldn't be accepted by people and that I shouldn't pursue it as a career. Even though I found something I truly loved, I was ready to give it up because of those inner dialogues from the fear of rejection.

Both social pressure and the fear of social rejection are rooted in our survival needs and can be very powerful in influencing our decisions. In ancient times, humans had to belong to a group to protect themselves from predators and have a mate to spread their genes to future generations. In those days, when it was very dangerous to live by oneself, social rejection almost equaled a death sentence. The times have changed, though, and there is far less physical danger now, but experiencing social rejection can still trigger various negative feelings, such as anxiety, insecurity, anger, sadness, depression, and low self-esteem. Research suggests the fear of social rejection can cause low performance at work, oversensitivity to potential threats, and a decrease in emotional intelligence. This is a fear that stops you from expressing your uniqueness and forces you to give up on your dreams.

The inner dialogues and the disempowering voices I heard about healing were coming from what I had learned from others throughout life. In a sense, those were the voices of my parents, teachers, neighbors, friends, colleagues, and ancestors. We refer to these ideas as common sense, norms, unspoken rules, biases, hidden assumptions, and so on. They are "collective beliefs" in society or any groups you belong to, whether it's a nation, company, religion, occupation, school, local community, project team, or even a small group of friends and families.

Examples of Disempowering Beliefs:

"I have to get married and start my family while I'm still young."

"I am too old to pursue my dreams."

"Higher education is only for rich people."

"We should live at a subsistence level."

"I have to have approval from my parents or siblings to make important decisions in my life."

Every group has a unique set of beliefs that shapes the norms and unspoken rules of the group. When you agree with such beliefs, you are accepted, and if not, you are exiled. Have you ever experienced this, perhaps during your adolescence in school? If you still carry pain from these times, social pressure can trigger inner dialogues that make you defensive and passive. To be accepted by your group, understanding and adhering to collective beliefs is important; it gives you a sense of belonging and safety in your social lives.

However, this "safety" is fake. It is given to you at the expense of your freedom to express yourself from your heart. A threat is built into this perceived safety; once you go against the socially accepted beliefs, you lose it. This is not real safety. How can you feel safe when you feel threatened underneath it all? How can you live your life fully without truly expressing yourself?

If you believe in an idea or a vision from your heart, it must be expressed. And if it goes against socially accepted beliefs, that's fine! Maybe it is an opportunity for the society or group to change. Instead of giving up your idea or vision and putting yourself in a victim mentality, you can stand up for your heart and spread your new ideas to others, so others can learn from you and evolve. This way, you can become a leader and an agent of change instead of a victim.

Martin Luther King, Jr. didn't settle for social norms. He stood up for what he believed in. He raised his voice, spread the word, and moved an entire society to consider his beliefs. There were many great leaders in history who challenged the collective's belief system and helped society evolve. They took on the challenge of shifting their entire group from a victim mindset to a leader mindset.

Many great ideas or visions were faced with unfavorable responses when they were first introduced to others. In the past, there was a time when fitness was not common. If you were running outside, people would say, "Who's chasing you?" In the mid 1990s, nobody wanted to buy things online because people believed they had to see the products in person. Before 2000, meditation was only for priests and religious people. Now, millions of people practice meditation every day, and businesses provide meditation spaces for their employees' well-being. Our societies need to continuously evolve and have the capacity to incorporate new ideas. You need to trust your heart and stand up for your vision.

Exercise: Social Pressures

1. Think back to a time when you gave up on something because of somebody else's opinion or social norms.

2. Ask yourself:

   Why is it so important for me to abide by societal norms?

   What do I need to go against those norms?

Becoming an Agent for Change

As we have discussed so far, starting something that is different from the norm is challenging because it triggers a fear of rejection from the society. This fear comes from our survival instincts, but is also enforced by traumatic experiences we endured during adolescence when we tried to fit in with a peer group. These experiences often cause people to become more susceptible to social pressure, and discourage people from expressing their deepest desires in their heart, putting them into a victim mentality. Generally, a victim mentality activates the worst version of you and makes your life miserable. This is not what your life is meant to look like.

Instead, you deserve to activate the best version of yourself, manifest your visions into reality, and make your life shine! Through the following discussions and exercises, you can heal those painful feelings from the past and empower yourself to conquer your fears, so you can become an agent of change in the society.

Embrace Your Uniqueness

John first met Diane at a party. They sat at the same table but didn't have anything to talk about. John wore a business suit, which made him look like a diligent businessman, while Diane had a hard-rock style. They both assumed they'd have no common interests to talk about. A few years later, when they met again at another party, Diane looked very different; she had changed to a more feminine style and spoke accordingly. John and Diane had a good time talking about various things, and naturally started dating. Eventually, they got married. Over their years of marriage, they had some challenging times, but they always managed to learn from each other, and grow, establishing mutual understanding, respect, and support for one another. They were able to respect each other's opinions and wish the other nothing but the best.

Then, one day, Diane made a confession to John. She had adopted a more feminine style when they started dating, to fit in with the social expectations of what a "good woman" or "good wife" should be or look like. In the past, when she had behaved as she wanted, many people had treated her harshly or even rejected her, and it was painful. But in her heart, she knew the "good wife" persona she had taken on was never her true nature. In fact, she had a rebellious spirit and felt the urge to change such social expectations of women. She had been suppressing her authentic desires, and it was killing her soul. She decided to embrace her true nature and express her uniqueness fully and completely.

John knew this day would come; he sensed it in her behaviors, and he also remembered the hard-rock style she had when they first met. He wondered how stressful it must have been for her to suppress her true nature. And he said, "Of course, I support you. Whatever makes you happy." After that conversation, Diane once again transformed herself; she shaved her hair on the sides, changed her clothes back to her hard-rock style, and altered her behaviors and the way she talked. She became happier and more energized, and John was happy to see her happier. The couple loved and trusted each other more than ever.

A few years later, Diane made another confession to John. She had fallen in love with a woman who worked with her, and she knew she wanted to spend her life with that person. John knew that, since childhood, she had been attracted to people's energy regardless of whether they were a man or

166

woman; therefore, he had been afraid this might happen. Did he get mad? No. Was he sad? Maybe. But when he looked at Diane who was expressing her apologies and asking for forgiveness, the only thing he wanted was for her to be happy. He thought to himself, "I cannot force her to stay with me. That does not make her happy, nor does it make a good marriage. The question is, would I support her decision even if we have to be separate?" The answer was clear. He said to Diane, "Don't worry; there is no need for apologies. I love you, and I support your decision because I want you to be happy." They got a divorce shortly after.

What happened to Diane after that was phenomenal. The relationship change served as the last step she needed to take to liberate her authenticity. She was able to tap into the true feelings in her heart, which enabled her to activate her creativity. She expressed her heightened creativity in the form of artistic jewelry products and made it into her own jewelry brand. Her jewelry products use only natural gemstones that are not polished nor curved, so the stones represent the owner as a symbol of their authenticity. Thus, her jewelry pieces became an inspiration for many people to embrace their uniqueness and live their life fully alive.

What happened to John? He changed so much too. Diane's way of life inspired John to live more outside of the box. He made a breakthrough in his business, and expanded his activities across many countries, which was beyond the comfort zone of social expectations. Diane and John still keep in touch, and surprisingly, they became the very best of friends and remain the biggest supporters of each other to this day.

Are you expressing your true nature, or are you suppressing some of your heart's desires? Because of social pressures, people tend to hide their desires or give them up completely, but it causes pain and builds up a lot of frustration inside. You ventured into this game of life to express what you have in your heart. Without expressing your true nature, who are you becoming?

If your true nature goes against social expectations, that's OK! Stop trying to be normal. Your true nature makes you unique from everybody else, and you can shine because of it. Embrace your uniqueness, express it fully and completely, and be proud of it. Liberate your authenticity. If somebody leaves you because you express your uniqueness, let them! You don't need it. That's basically them saying, "I'll only like you if you hide your true self." This is not a relationship based on true love, is it? You deserve better relationships, and you will attract true love by expressing who you truly are. True love stays with you always, whether it's with a partner, family, friends, or colleagues. They love you and support you no matter what, even if you have a difference in opinions.

Perhaps you had painful experiences where people treated you harshly when you went against social expectations. J.K. Rowling got rejected by twelve publishers for her *Harry Potter* series because they feared that a book written by a female author wouldn't appeal to boys. Oprah Winfrey was fired from her first job at a TV station because the producer decided she was "unfit for television news." Well, these women proved them very wrong, as we all know. When you are confronted by social norms, you should not stop. That's when you are supposed to jump! It's so important to heal any past emotional pain you may have, so you can empower yourself to make your visions come true.

Exercise: Healing Judgments

1. Think of a moment when you were judged, criticized, or rejected by others. Imagine listening to your past self's feelings, thoughts, and emotions.

2. When they're finished, embrace him/her with a hug.

3. Say to yourself:

It doesn't matter what others think about me.

I am safe, protected, and loved.

Nothing can stop me from becoming who I am meant to be.

I have everything I need to create the life I want.

Ask yourself: What did I learn from this?

Exercise: Embrace Uniqueness

1. Think of the characters from your favorite movie, and how each of them was portrayed to be unique, precious, and an important part of the story.

2. Imagine watching your life as a movie, with many unique individuals playing roles.

3. Ask yourself: How can I make my life more colorful by expressing my uniqueness?

Drop Attachment

In 2009, I managed the Japan operation of a meditative healing technique. The technique was growing, but our audience was still small; therefore, my focus was on increasing people's awareness of the technique. To accomplish this goal, we did a series of marketing campaigns—publications of books, ads on social networking sites, and interview articles with celebrities in magazines, newspapers, and on the radio. It was a lot of work, but I believed it was essential in making a positive impression of the healing technique for a broader audience in Japan.

However, some practitioners in the meditative healing community didn't like it. From their perspective, the marketing campaign was commercializing the sacred nature of the healing technique and deteriorating the purity of the teaching. They believed we should not make it a business. I understood how they felt, but I disagreed with their perspective. Even if the technique was very good, we needed to bring the information to an audience so they could be motivated to come to healing practitioners. Also, to deliver healing activity continuously, we had to make it work financially too, and business was a vehicle through which we could continuously deliver the act of love to a broad audience so that society as a whole could benefit. Besides, the idea of marketing was not my sole decision, it was a joint effort with the founder of the healing technique.

I wanted to talk to the practitioners who were opposed to the marketing campaign and ask for their support, but they never spoke to me directly. Instead, they spread hurtful misinformation about me in their classes, and on their blogs and social networking profiles. This made me angry, and I was tempted to fight back, but I didn't. I knew that fighting back would aggravate the situation, and I didn't want to express a low-vibrational version of myself. Besides, I couldn't change their opinion unless they were open to discussion. I decided to let go of my attachment to "fix them" so I could better focus on doing a good job with the marketing campaign.

Within a couple of years, the effects from the marketing campaign were obvious to everyone. We had a lot more people receiving healings from us, a lot more people coming to learn the technique, and a thriving community. And yet, we maintained the purity of the teaching; the concerns of some practitioners did not come true. We succeeded in creating a great momentum.

I wondered how the people who attacked me were seeing this. I looked through their pictures on social media, and I was glad to find that they looked so happy having a lot more students in their classes. When I met them at a party, they approached me and spoke to me as if nothing had happened, commending me on the success of the marketing campaign. To my surprise, they changed their perspective, and they became nicer than ever!

It is natural for people to have different opinions. We can respect each other's opinions and still maintain good relationships. But it's unfortunate when someone responds negatively to your authentic expression, and that might hurt your feelings. However, you cannot force them to change. Perhaps they have a traumatic memory that triggers negative behaviors, but that has nothing to do with you. They need to heal their trauma and change their beliefs and perspectives. That is their responsibility, not yours. You are not responsible for fixing others. Everyone is equipped with the capacity to change themselves, if they need to. If you chase after them and try to prove yourself or fix them, you will waste tremendous energy and distract yourself from the important work in front of you. So, I advise you to drop the attachment and the need to prove yourself or fix others and focus on what you do best instead.

Exercise: Drop Attachment

1. Think back to a time when people rejected you because of your uniqueness, ideas, or vision.

2. Ask yourself: Does it really matter to prove them wrong? What can I put my energy into instead?

Gratitude

Masha was an executive coach in a leadership training company that offered private coaching, as well as coaching-based trainings in workshops, supporting participants in better managing their businesses. Ever since she joined the company, she dreamed of starting her own training business to empower people in different countries, and she shared her vision with her colleagues. Over the years, she earned a good reputation as a trainer, her classes grew larger, and her activities expanded outside of the company to make keynote speeches in large conferences. With increased confidence, she decided to leave the company and start her own training business to fulfill her dreams.

When Masha quit the company and started her own training business, all of her colleagues were happy with her decision and offered support. Her boss, Carlos, however, was not happy. Masha's classes were attracting many participants, and it was a major loss to the company without them. Also, Carlos was concerned that Masha might take clients from the company to her new business. To address potential problems, Carlos had meetings with every colleague Masha had worked with in the company, and dug for any suspicious activity or behavior from her, notifying them of the possible consequences for misconduct from Masha or any colleagues involved. This discouraged colleagues from supporting Masha proactively; they all stopped responding to her communications, whether it was through e-mail, text, social media, or phone calls. The company planned to issue an announcement about her departure for her new business, but that was cancelled. The company designated one of Masha's closest colleagues to take over her workload. Large conferences cancelled her keynote speeches for no reason. In just a short period of time, all traces of Masha in the company disappeared; it was as if she had never existed. She did not anticipate any of this, but she understood why the company had to do it. Nevertheless, it made her sad.

On the other hand, her business was not going well. Her own training programs were drawing in only a few participants for every class, and she was losing money. This was the time she needed support from her ex-colleagues the most, but they all stopped communicating with her. She realized how essential it had been to receive support in the previous company. More than anything, she missed the connection with her colleagues and participants, the people who supported her for years. She had been driven by her desire to make her own business successful, but she realized that it didn't mean anything without anyone to share the success with. She lost everything. She didn't know what to do. She was disappointed, lonely, and helpless.

After a while, she decided to accept the situation and surrender. She stopped trying to control the situation but started to go with the flow instead, enjoying every experience and doing her best, hoping to make it better little by little, find people to support her, and build her own customer base from the ground up. To her surprise, some colleagues started contacting her; they were worried about her and were willing to offer support. Some participants from the past found her on the internet and joined her new classes.

Then, something interesting happened. After going through a period of sadness from the lack of connection with others, every connection became precious for her, and she started to feel a lot of gratitude for every single person who came into her life. This feeling of gratitude toward everyone was something she had never felt before. There still weren't a ton of people coming into her life, but Masha felt very grateful and happy to have them because they were coming to her for her heart, not because of benefits, necessity, or out of obligation. She was grateful to the previous company for the lessons and connections it had given her in the past. Her classes were still small, but she was grateful for every single participant who shared their precious time with her. By simply connecting with the gratitude in her heart, she experienced the utmost joy and pleasure. Every day, she experienced fulfillment of her heartfelt desire, which was somewhat different from the worldly definition of business success.

As Masha publicly communicated her joy and gratitude, many people were touched and regarded her classes as "gratitude teachings." Word spread and her classes attracted like-minded people, and eventually, her teaching grew very well as a business, too. After several years, her teaching spread to other countries, and she realized her vision "to empower people in different countries" had been manifested into reality, but there was something about it she didn't anticipate. Her business didn't teach executives how to better manage their businesses; instead, it taught everyone how to live with joy and gratitude. Now, she is full of gratitude for the company, people, and even the difficult times she went through when she first started her business. Certainly, she was guided to her destiny, which was beyond her imagination.

When you make a change in your life, it'll most likely impact others in some way. Sometimes people react out of fear and leave your life. Sometimes things do not go as you anticipated, and you might go through difficult times. In such turbulent times, it's important to drop your desire to control everything and respond with gratitude instead. Be grateful for the people who spend time with you, the things that are supporting you, and the challenges that are teaching you something. And when you keep expressing gratitude to others and the universe, you will inevitably receive gratitude back, and then everything that happens in your life will guide you to the destination you seek.

Exercise: Gratitude

1. Think of the people you see every day.

2. For each person, think of a quality in them that you are grateful for.

3. In your imagination, say to the person: "Thank you for being in my life."

A Leader Is Born!

As we discussed, when you have an idea, vision, or desire that goes against social expectations, you might experience some challenges that tempt you to give up on your ideas and yourself. However, the experience of social pressure helps you conquer your fears and activate confidence, courage, and commitment to transform yourself into a leader that brings positive change to the society you belong to. The key to getting through these challenges includes embracing your uniqueness, focusing on your vision by dropping attachment to prove yourself, and experiencing joy by appreciating everything in your life. With pure intention to be of service to others, the trajectory of your energy adjusts its course to cross paths with your destiny, which allows you to shine at your brightest for others.

Exercise: A leader is born!

1. Imagine you are taking on a new project with your unique ideas and visions, and others are supporting you. How do you feel in your heart?

2. Ask yourself:
    What values would I be creating in society?
    How would I be inspiring others?

STAGE 4. COLLABORATION

Why Do We Compete?

Many years ago, I used to work for an investment bank in New York, offering IT solutions for Japanese businesses. I was in close proximity to the competitive work environment of Wall Street back in those days. I remember I was amazed by the way stockbrokers got compensated according to their performance. There were many people who received millions of dollars in bonuses, some of them more than ten million dollars. At one time, there was a man who received thirty million dollars in bonuses. I was very surprised to hear the news because I knew that the man did not do physically hard work at all. Every day, he seemed to have nothing to do; he just looked at a computer screen and thought to himself, refraining from interacting with others.

Later, I learned he was responsible for making computer programs, or algorithms, to be used for stock trading that generated maximum profits in every trade. The company contracted him and agreed to pay him a portion of the profit from every transaction, which totaled thirty million dollars at the end of the year. If I were him, I would be happy with thirty million dollars, quit the job for good, and go on vacation, but he didn't quit. He continued what he did and made fifty million dollars the following year. Someone asked him how much he had in his bank account, and he said, "I don't have a lot left in my bank account. I am spending a lot of money. You know, when you make a lot of money, you make friends with people who spend a lot of money, and you end up needing more money to hang out with them. I need to keep making more money every year."

While the company paid some employees a lot of money, there were many who needed to leave the company because of their poor performance. I remember a man who was in charge of the computer networks in the company. One day, he made a mistake in configuring one of the network devices, which caused the company to lose a half-million dollars. A couple of hours after the incident, he was called into his boss's office and was fired. "Don't bother returning to your desk. Don't talk to anyone. We'll send your belongings later," his boss said. He seemed to be upset but didn't say anything back; he just walked away. The entire episode—from the network outage to the firing—took place within a few hours. It was terrifying for me to watch people get kicked out of the company. I felt he was treated without honor or respect for all the good work he had done, and I thought, "There is something terribly wrong about this."

The company ranked employees based on their performance and determined their compensation accordingly. Of course, those at the bottom of the ranking got fired every quarter. Naturally, employees were nervous about their position in the ranking, which caused them to act out of fear. It was ridiculous, but those behaviors were somewhat childish and harsh—bullying, backstabbing, interfering, stealing, hiding, and so on. One year, the company's sales decreased significantly, and the executives needed to make major budget cuts. The management hired a senior executive and put him in charge of cutting costs, and of course, the main way to cut the most costs was to fire as many employees as possible. This period of "aggressive firing" was a nightmare. The new executive announced that all teams in the company needed to reduce their manpower to its minimum, but the way he demanded it was a lot more aggressive than "minimum"—he called it "bare bones". As a result, many talented employees were let go, and at the end of the year, the executive successfully reduced a large amount of costs, but he was still a couple million dollars short of the company's expectations. What happened to him? The company fired him to reach the company's cost reduction target.

Unfortunately, competitive behavior is not unique to Wall Street. It is worshipped in many areas of our society, including education, sports, and business. When I started my healing business in 2008, I was disappointed to experience competition among healing practitioners who were supposed to be operating out of love. Back then, the market for healing businesses was small. Every business proactively promoted its services, which was normal, but eventually, businesses began competing with each other. When they saw another healing business attracting more customers, they got jealous, blamed the other business for taking away their customers, and spread horrible rumors about them. Back then, I was running my business very well and received jealous reactions from other businesses. They sent me emails blaming me for their misfortune, said terrible things about me behind my back, and posted false rumors on social media. This damaged my reputation and hurt my feelings; it made me sad because they used to be my close friends. We used to get together and dream about our visions; we had promised to support each other. And yet, when my business grew, they reacted differently. I asked myself, *do I need to give up my friendships to succeed?*

As I recall these situations, there were some beliefs that influenced our behaviors in such a competitive environment:

- Results determine the value of a person.

- There is not enough for everyone.

- More is better.

- We have to win over others to survive.

- The winner thrives at the expense of the losers.

These beliefs are prevalent in our society. Since birth, we were raised in environments that perpetuated these beliefs. Everyone acted according to these beliefs, including our parents, family members, friends, and teachers. These are unspoken assumptions in schools, in movies and TV programs, and in sporting events. Our definition of money, success, and happiness are based on these beliefs. However, are these absolute truths? Does this help create happiness in our society?

The root of all these beliefs comes from our survival instincts, justified by saying "survival of the fittest." When humans lived in caves, we were exposed to physical threats from predators and needed to fight to survive. We also needed to battle against other communities that attempted to conquer our own. We became sensitive to potential threats and increased our physical strength to respond to them, which helped us survive and prosper. The operating principle was that either we win everything or lose everything. We were driven by fears—our fear of losing everything, the fear of starvation, the fear of death, and the fear of uncertainty. Today, many of us no longer have physical threats to worry about, but we still carry these beliefs and fears, which influence our desire for significance by means of superiority, power, money, material possessions, respect, social status, and a higher quality of life. A threat to our significance triggers agitation and causes anger, resentment, and jealousy. There is an enormous amount of energy within these feelings, and they empower us to perform hostile behaviors against others, pushing others aside so we can rise higher.

The quest for significance and superiority is a never-ending battle because no matter how much you acquire, there is always somebody else who will have more, and you will never get the satisfaction you desire. Because you fight only for your own benefit and push aside others, you build up emotional barriers against others and fail to establish deep connections. Therefore, even if you attain significance and superiority, it will be at the expense of happiness. How can you be truly happy without deep connections with others?

When some people are severely defeated in competition, they give up on themselves and allow fear to rule their life. They feel powerless and hopeless, and become depressive. They put themselves in a victim mentality, spending their life complaining, whining, and self-pitying. This makes for a very difficult experience, but it is also a great opportunity to overcome the fears, get out of the illusion of "survival of the fittest," and redirect their lives to a higher purpose. To do so, they need to heal the pain from their past, conquer their fears, and reconnect with their inner resources to create whatever reality they wish.

As you conquer your fears and release the desire for significance, you will be able to participate in any competition with a totally different energy. You will no longer compete with others; rather, you will compete with yourself. Your intention will be to increase your level of excellence to bring out your best in competitions, and you will use others to increase your motivation, embracing your differences and aiming for higher excellence. With this mindset, a competition becomes a collaborative effort to bring out the highest possible expression of our being. This is what I call "healthy competition". We can find many such examples in some top athletes. For example, the rivalry between Cristiano Ronaldo and Lionel Messi in professional football in Spain pushed the two athletes to a level of mastery one couldn't have attained without the other. After leaving Spain, Cristiano said that his longtime rivalry with Lionel made him "a better player". If you have somebody you can compete with in a healthy way, it is a gift from the universe to help you reach higher excellence. Even if it is presented as a competition, it is a collaboration in its essence, and the experience can be deeply satisfying for both of your souls.

You ventured into this game of life to grow spiritually, help others grow, and enjoy physical experiences. You can work on your mission by yourself and do a lot of great things in life, but you can make even greater things through collaboration. This is the important key behind large successes, whether it's in business, sports, or any other activity. When you join forces with others who share the same vision, your energy amplifies and your vision expands even more, and together, you can create an unstoppable momentum that manifests the shared vision into reality. This way, you can experience the utmost joy and fulfillment with other souls and make a major difference in the society.

Exercise: Competition

1. Try to imagine the moment your soul returns to the spiritual realm, and all your material possessions, achievements, and fame are left behind. You now exist as a soul—a pure consciousness—in a world of infinite time and space.

2. Ask yourself: As a soul, what is more important for me than competing with others?

Fear of Attack

Annette was so happy and proud when she was appointed as the representative of an executive coaching technique to oversee its certified coaches in her region. She had earned this position; she had built a good reputation as a highly regarded coach in her region and took on the responsibility of promoting the technique to top executives in the region. 'Regional Representative' was a newly created role, and there were a lot of uncertainties, but she was committed to leading the community of coaches and making a positive impact on the society. Her peer coaches congratulated her on her new role and expressed their excitement; many of them offered support, as well as requests on how to manage the community—establishing rules, protocols, roles, and responsibilities, marketing proactively, addressing training needs, and so on. She was happy to receive these requests, as it showed that everyone wanted to make the organization successful. Her first big project in the new role was to invite the founder of the coaching method to the region and organize a series of workshops for local coaches.

When she opened registration for the workshops, she was puzzled. The sign-up was very slow—only a few registrations every day. All the planned workshops were popular ones, and many people had been asking for the workshops for years, but only a small number of people were signing up. "What's going on!?" she wondered. Anette and her team spoke to other coaches, asking them why they were not signing up, and found out the reason. Alejandro—a very popular and respected coach in the region—and his big number of followers weren't interested in the workshops that year. They were not happy with Annette taking the representative role and were spreading rumors about her, saying she was not qualified for the position because of her lack of experience and skill, and her focus on commercialization. They believed Annette was discounting the original values of the technique by commercializing it too much. They believed Annette should resign immediately, and Alejandro should take over the position, and they wouldn't participate in the workshops until it happened.

This was shocking for Annette. She thought everyone was happy about her taking the role, but that was not the case. She had learned from Alejandro in the past, and she respected his teaching and contribution to the community. She was aware that he had a lot more coaching experience and skill than she did, but she wanted to contribute what she did best, delivering pure teachings to a broader audience through marketing. Besides, the representative role was the founder's decision, not hers. Her taking the role was a surprise for her too. She was also shocked that her peer coaches were against her. They studied with her, and they had been good friends, but now, they were against her. She thought they were happy and would be supportive, but they weren't. Annette realized she had lost contact with her closest friends, and was sad when she discovered that all of them were leaving her. With these thoughts, she felt deep pain in her heart; she felt attacked, sad, lonely, and somewhat guilty. Why guilty? Because she took the role away from her teacher, Alejandro, even though it was not her intention to do so.

That's when she came to me for advice. I had dealt with many similar situations in the past, and had experienced both sides. When I was in Annette's shoes in other situations, I felt disappointed, attacked, and alone, so I understood her pain very well. I worked with her to change the situation for the better.

Firstly, I had to help Annette realize she had done nothing wrong. She had been working for the benefit of the community of coaches and the society, and the founder wanted her to continue to make those same contributions in a leadership position, which required more of a management approach than a coaching one. This was not to discredit other coaches, nor was it supposed to make her superior to others. It was unfortunate that some people didn't like the decision, but it was the founder's call, not hers. She could stand up tall and be proud of her role without guilt.

What was causing the most pain for her was this feeling of guilt. Normally, she was intelligent enough to be able to push away all the offensive reactions from others with effective reasoning and compassion. But the feeling of guilt was showing her the illusion that everyone was leaving her— causing her to feel sad and alone.

The feeling of guilt was coming from a painful experience she had had during her school days, when her female classmates were jealous of her popularity among boys because of her appearance. She was left alone back then and had no girls to talk to, and she had experienced sadness and loneliness. She felt guilty because she didn't believe she was deserving of popularity. With nobody else to talk to and rely on in school, she did everything by herself and studied hard. Over the years, she performed very well academically, and became an independent and capable person at an early age. As she remembered all these things, she realized that the feelings of guilt and loneliness had been motivating her to work and study hard. She decided she didn't need them anymore, and let go of those negative feelings.

Secondly, there was no need to do anything. Annette didn't need to do anything for the people who were reacting negatively to her new role. If she tried to confront and respond to them negatively, it would aggravate the situation. Everyone deserved to have their opinions. If they could not support the founder's decision, it was their problem, not hers. Those negative behaviors were triggered by their fear, and there were lessons for them to learn. The situation was giving them an opportunity to learn and grow, and there was nothing Annette could do about it. She also needed to understand that their negative behaviors were not their true nature. Once they learned their lessons, they would come back to who they truly were, and be her friends again. Some people might learn quickly, others might take more time, and some might take their lifetimes to learn. That's OK. Everyone has their own learning curve. What she could do was trust that everyone had the capacity to learn their lessons by themselves and would be back to being nicer people someday.

Thirdly, the best thing she could do was to lead by a vision. Instead of confronting Alejandro and his followers, she could lead the community by showing them a future vision and promoting the need for collaboration, so they could have a shared purpose and work together. If she would like, she could invite Alejandro to collaborate with her as an example others could follow. That way, she could help the community grow beyond competition and establish collaboration so they could grow together as one team. That would guide the community in the right direction.

Exercise: Healing the Fear of Attack

1. Think back to a time when you were attacked by someone physically, verbally, or in any other way. Hug yourself as you were then, and say, "It's OK. You are safe. I am here for you. I love you."

2. Imagine a beautiful sunshine beyond the clouds of negative thoughts and emotions in your mind.

3. Say to yourself: I am strong, magnificent, powerful, and invincible.

4. Ask yourself: What kind of relationships do I want in my life instead?

Jealousy

Alejandro had mixed feelings when Annette was appointed as the representative of the executive coaching technique. Yes, Annette was doing well in her business, but she was still a junior to Alejandro, and he didn't see the qualities of a leader in her. In addition, he was concerned that Annette might focus too much on making money and lose sight of maintaining the purity of the coaching method, thereby giving a wrong impression to the general public.

On the other hand, Alejandro had been working hard for years to spread the technique from the ground up, and he had trained almost all the experienced coaches in the region, including Annette. He didn't understand why the founder chose Annette over him. Considering his past contributions, he should be the one to take the role, not Annette. He got angry and resentful because it was like Annette took the position away from him. He was also jealous that the founder chose Annette over him; it was as if the founder liked her better. He said to himself, "Annette must have done something to deceive the founder to take this role." He felt the decision was unfair and wrong, and he felt disappointed, disrespected, ignored, and even abandoned.

Alejandro's followers were disappointed, too. They were angry at Annette for taking the position away from him; they felt the decision disrespected their teacher. They could not accept Annette as a leader because they thought she did not have enough experience or skill. These feelings clouded the judgment of Alejandro and his followers, and now, they only searched for information to support their feelings, filtering out all other information that proved otherwise. Whatever Annette did, Alejandro and his followers would never want to participate in it. They started talking to the founder directly to change the decision and put Alejandro in Annette's position.

Then, the founder came to me for advice. When I was in Alejandro's shoes in other situations, I was disappointed and felt insulted, abandoned, disrespected, so I understood his pain very well. I worked with him through the founder to change the situation for the better.

Firstly, Alejandro had done nothing wrong. His contribution to the community was well regarded by the founder and everyone. On the other hand, Annette had done nothing wrong either. Her contribution to the expansion of the audience through marketing was well regarded too. It was the founder's decision to appoint Annette for the representative role because of her dedication in driving the growth of the community. It was not to discredit Alejandro in any way; the level of respect and gratitude the founder had for him did not change.

Secondly, Alejandro needed to heal his pain. I asked him when he first felt those same feelings, and after contemplation, he realized those feelings were coming from his experience as a child, when he was around five to ten years old. Back then, his father always favored his brother, Carlos, and didn't give him much attention. Even when Alejandro worked hard and did well in school, his father still didn't spend much time with him, and favored Carlos instead. This made Alejandro feel disappointed, disrespected, ignored, and abandoned. In those days, he always had to compete against his brother to gain the attention of his father, and he lost it again and again. He said to himself, "No matter how well I do, it's not enough for others to love me." This motivated him to work even harder in his studies at school, and later, it helped him achieve a lot in his professional life as well, although his fear of being disrespected by others lingered.

As he spoke to me, he started to remember the good memories of how he was respected, recognized, and appreciated by others. He received honorable awards, and he had many followers. Then, he realized he didn't need to worry about being respected anymore. He was loved so much already for who he was, regardless of his achievements, fame, or position. It was meaningless to be jealous of Annette for taking the leadership role because there was nothing he would miss or lose. With that awareness, the feelings of disappointment, disrespect, and abandonment melted away in his heart, and he was able to forgive Annette, his father and brother, and himself for staying stuck in that illusion of fear for so long. This time, he said to himself, "I am loved by everyone. I do not need to compete anymore. I am free from the fear of losing love."

Thirdly, Alejandro had to drop the habit of competition. The idea of people fighting over a position was meaningless in light of the higher purpose of the community to do good deeds in the society. Alejandro had been working for the community, and so was Annette. They were allies working together toward the same goal. I asked him, "Is it constructive to continue competing? Or is it better to collaborate and make something big together?" Of course, the answer was the latter. He decided to drop the ego's desire for significance, be a bigger person, support the founder's decision, and focus on collaborating with everyone in the community. Then, he understood that Annette would be the best talent in growing the community, and he became happy for her and more willing to cooperate and collaborate with her. In releasing his past hurt, he was able to commit to becoming a great example of collaboration and be the change he wished to see in the world.

Exercise: Healing Jealousy

1. Think back to a time when you felt jealous of someone.

2. Imaging hugging yourself, and say: "It's OK. You are safe. I am here for you. I love you. You are special, precious, and valuable. You are free."

3. Imagine a beautiful sunshine beyond the clouds of the negative thoughts and emotions in your mind.

4. Say to yourself: I can create anything I want in my life. All I need is within me now.

5. Ask yourself: What would be the best version of me that truly shines?

Collaboration and Prosperity

Many of us have been participating in competitions and investing enormous amounts of energy in the form of stress, nervousness, worry, anger, jealousy, or despair. Suppose you can change all of this, how would you like to experience your energy instead? The most meaningful way to experience your energy is by aligning your energy with a vision that resonates with your heart, and gives you happiness, joy, and fulfillment. Further, what if you had people in your life who shared your vision and worked with you? By joining forces with them, the energy will increase exponentially, and the vision will expand for the benefit of many others. This is how we can create prosperity in our lives. Take a moment to visualize what you want in your heart and manifest your prosperity.

Exercise: Collaboration and Prosperity

1. Imagine all your competitors becoming your allies. They act on a principle of "one for all, all for one," collaborating for a shared vision and goal.

2. Ask yourself: What can be possible with this kind of team?

STAGE 5. ABUNDANCE

What Is Abundance?

Abundance means having more than enough of something, but this definition invites various interpretations. What does abundance mean to you?

In the past, before I started meditation and healing activities, abundance meant having more than enough money and material possessions, and I believed those things would make me happy. Therefore, I was motivated to acquire nice clothes, a car, a residence, and money. When I turned thirty and had acquired all such material conditions for happiness, I realized they did not make me happy, at least not in my heart. Sure, I had many things and money in my life, which represented a higher quality of life on the outside, but I didn't feel like my inner self had a high quality of life. If monetary abundance did not make me happy, what did it imply? There was something fundamentally wrong with my definition of abundance.

In my quest for "real abundance," I first realized the desires for material possessions were coming from fears. For example, I was afraid of becoming inferior to others; therefore, I wanted to have nice clothes, a car, and a residence to look better. I wanted to travel overseas to have nicer experiences than others. I was afraid of what might happen in the future because I didn't have confidence in myself, so I wanted to have a lot of money to maintain my quality of life. However, as we discussed in prior chapters, these fear-based desires were illusions. I didn't need to compare myself to others, and I didn't need to worry about my future. Everything I needed was within me, and those qualities are infinitely and eternally available.

Now, here's a big question. When I let go of all those fears and illusions, what would I want for myself instead? I learned the answer in a strange way. Several years ago, I received a message from a very wealthy man, saying he would give me a donation of ten million dollars. He said he was dying and would like to use his money for good purposes. I was surprised but graciously accepted the offer. As I was arranging the administrative details with him, I started fantasizing about how I'd use the money—move to a better office, hire talented employees, invest in a larger project, or give money to my family and friends as a sign of gratitude. I realized, at that moment, that all my fears were gone, and I was visualizing all these ideas out of pure joy and happiness, activating good intentions in myself, achieving higher excellence in my business, creating opportunities for others, offering better service to others, expressing gratitude, and so on. I noticed my shoulders were relaxed, my lungs were breathing more easily, and my heart was wide open. But later, after I completed a background check on the wealthy man, I learned the person did not exist; it was a scam! I was shocked and disappointed, of course, but I did not get angry because I was still in that state of joy and fulfillment, fantasizing about everything I wanted without any fear; it was such an amazing feeling. I decided then and there that I should maintain that amazing feeling without needing to wait for a large amount of money to come, and I should trust myself and work on all those great ideas. So, the answer to the question was, when I let go of those fears and illusions, I would experience higher virtuous qualities in my life by gaining higher excellence, being of better service to others, and expressing lots of gratitude. The absence of fear activated those virtuous qualities in myself, and I experienced such a joyful feeling.

So, what is abundance? Here's my definition in light of the Game of Life Theory. Abundance is a state of mind to believe that there are more than enough resources to activate the highest qualities in yourself, others, and everything around you. For example, I experience abundance when I see my healing clients transform into a resourceful state and when their faces light up with beautiful smiles during a private session. I experience abundance when I am touched by someone's story. I have many friends who are so kind and supportive of me, and they activate my confidence and courage, which is abundance. I experience abundance in my cozy residence because it gives me peace, comfort, and relaxation. Visiting the Grand Canyon is always an abundant experience to me because of its magnificence and wonder.

These higher qualities are some of the many aspects of the highest possible presence in the universe—God, Creator of All That Is, or whatever you call it. As we discussed earlier, we all are on a soul journey to get back to our origin, God's presence. As part of the journey, you ventured into this game of life to grow and experience a physical world. Abundance is a way of life to embrace and appreciate all that exists in the world and to see God's qualities in yourself, every living being, and every inanimate object, knowing there is more than enough for everyone and everything to express its highest potential.

When you experience abundance, you attract more abundance. That is the Law of Attraction. If you feel elegance by looking at beautiful flowers, you attract more of that elegance into your life. When you enjoy high-quality surroundings in your life, things like a comfortable sofa, relaxing lights from the fireplace, and a warm blanket, you attract more of those qualities of comfort, relaxation, and warmth. When you do something kind for somebody, you receive kindness from another. If you experience joy and gratitude by giving, you will attract that same energy through receiving.

These are the moments and opportunities that activate your higher virtuous qualities, bringing out the best version of you. What exactly you attract depends on what events, objects, or people you feel have high qualities. If abundance to you means having higher qualities of peace and warmth in your life, you will attract whatever makes you feel peace and warmth; perhaps it's a calm neighborhood, friendly neighbors, and a comfortable sofa. But if you determine that your abundance is about having elegance and perfection, perhaps you will attract things like luxurious residences, high-quality clothes, and people with elegant demeanors and high integrity. Of course, you can determine what abundance means to you to include all of these and a lot more. You can experience abundance in your own way.

Exercise: Abundance

1. Think of a time when you experienced the highest and best version of yourself.

2. Ask yourself:
   What qualities were present?
   What enabled me to embody those qualities?

Knowing

It is essential to know that abundance is the true nature of life. Even if the things you possess today seem limited, they do not determine your future. What really matters is your inner quality because your external life is a reflection of your inner life. You can manifest what you want in your life with the power of your inner qualities, and they are infinitely available. When you are in a difficult situation, your material possessions are not what give you a solution—it is your qualities such as creativity and resourcefulness that solve the problem. When you are aiming for a challenging goal, it's not your skills or physical abilities that determine the outcome, but it is your inner strength, confidence, and perseverance that get you through the challenge and defy the odds to make things happen.

If you ever felt your life was controlled by other people or your environment, it is not true. Material things do not drive your life; your inner qualities do. If you accept that you are a victim of your environment, it will work out that way. But if you determine that you always have the choice and the power to change the status quo for the better, you can be the creator of something great in your life. You simply need to activate your creative qualities within and have a vision for what you want to create for yourself.

To activate an inner quality, you must simply remember the moment you experienced the quality before. For example, you can remember a time when you felt the strongest and the most confident, to bring out those feelings in the present moment and use them to deal with the situation in front of you. Again, these qualities are infinite. Does your kindness run out if you are kind to others many times? No. Is your imagination limited by the physical space of your mind? No. There is no limitation on space nor time in your mind. There is no limitation to your imagination and any other inner qualities.

Sometimes you need to activate qualities you've never experienced before. You can still bring out the quality by learning from someone else's story through a book, movie or by listening to somebody talk. Have you ever felt strong and vibrant after watching an action movie? Have you ever felt love and compassion after watching a romantic movie? When you learn higher virtuous qualities from someone else's experience, you can feel them, and it activates the same qualities in you. As you practice demonstrating these qualities in your life, you can embody them as yours, and they'll become part of you.

You have all the virtuous qualities available within yourself, and they are infinitely and eternally available. They are the real resources you use to create whatever you want in your life. You have all the resources you need, and they are more than enough. That is the true nature of life.

Co-Creation

As quantum physics discovered, everything has potentials of various qualities waiting to be expressed. The moment an observer chooses what quality to observe, it gets expressed accordingly. In other words, the qualities to be expressed by an object in front of you depend on what you choose to observe in that object. In that sense, you are co-creating reality with the object.

Let's say you have a car you've owned for the past ten years. You say to yourself, *Oh, this car is getting old. It is noisy and almost falling apart.* As you start the engine, your thought is confirmed by the unstable noise from the engine and the shaking movement of the car. But the next day, someone you trust tells you your car is amazing, stable, and strong, even after ten years, and it will stay useful for another ten years. Then, your attention shifts, and you start noticing the stability and strength of the car.

Your experiences are influenced by what you choose to observe or pay attention to. At every moment, you are co-creating your reality with everything around you, and this also applies to humans. Let's say you have an employee who recently made a mistake and performed poorly. When meeting with this person as his/her manager, you might have had the temptation to blame them for their mistake, but you knew it would not help the situation at all. Instead, you chose to start the conversation by saying, "I know you have high integrity and precision, and are capable of great work. I am grateful to have you on my team, but the recent incident did not demonstrate these qualities. What might be some ways in which you can keep performing at your best?" By indicating the good qualities in that person, you are helping him/her draw out those good qualities to help solve the situation, instead of bringing up their fear-based qualities that cause them to defend themselves.

Everything has potential of expressing itself in different ways in every moment, and you have a choice and the power to draw what you want from your environment. Your choice as an observer determines the expression of an object/person, and filters out all other possibilities.

Unfortunately, people make this choice subconsciously, on autopilot. Subconscious choices are made based on the beliefs and perspectives you've learned from your environment, and they do not necessarily serve you well. If you believe someone is mean because of a rumor, you automatically choose to observe the mean aspect of the person, and that draws out their "mean" nature. In this instance, your experiences have gone on autopilot. Unless you consciously stop this, you will keep letting your beliefs and perspectives drive your reality, based on what you learned from your parents, family, teachers, friends, and so forth.

With autopilot, you can still experience abundance by surrounding yourself with people and things you believe are expressing higher qualities, so that they activate higher qualities in you. For example, you can wear nice clothes to experience elegance, integrity, and comfort; you can travel overseas to experience the wonder and magnificence of nature; and you can make investments or donations and experience the joy and fulfillment of utilizing your financial resources for the benefit of others. In this way, material possessions and money can be good tools to activate and express your higher qualities; however, this abundance is limited. You cannot get out of the confinement of your beliefs and perspectives when you co-create on autopilot. When you encounter things and people you don't like in your belief system, you will draw out their lower vibrations and thereby activate your own lower qualities—such as stress, anger, hatred, or rejection. This will immediately push you out of the abundance experience.

To keep experiencing abundance in your life, you need to stop running on autopilot, and consciously co-create your reality. This does not have to be hard; it simply means choosing to see the good in everything and everyone that comes your way. By seeing good qualities in others, you allow such qualities to come out in you. You can practice this by seeing good qualities in virtually everything you encounter. For example, let's say you are jogging outside, and it starts to rain. You might typically say, "Oh my god, this rain ruins my day!" But instead, you can choose to see the bright side of the rain, and say, "Thanks to the rain, my body will chill out nicely, there will be less people on the road, and I can run faster and have more joy than ever." Blue skies give you a refreshing feeling, beautiful flowers cheer you up, squirrels in the park show you examples of swiftness, and the sunshine that comes through the leaves on the trees encourages you to do what you love in your life.

Even when you cannot change the physical aspects of your environment, you can change the values you see in them. The value, meaning, and qualities of situations are a reflection of your choice as an observer, and they influence the quality of your internal life. If you can see higher qualities in the things and people around you, it gives you a feeling of abundance, and you'll be able to attract more of the same energy in your life. As you keep growing spiritually, you can choose to see 'good' in more things and people around you, which helps you experience more abundance in your life.

Act of Giving

The act of giving amplifies the abundance in your life. It activates many virtuous qualities and gives you the joy of experiencing the best version of you.

For example, sometimes we experience difficult challenges in our lives. It's not easy to stay positive when you encounter situations, like health challenges, losing a job or business, being in a miserable relationship, or losing loved ones. When you see someone going through such difficult situations, you can offer support. You can sit down with the person and listen, cry with them, or give them a hug. You can share some food or drinks, give gifts, or even offer financial support, if it's appropriate. Money might not buy happiness, but it can help solve problems in its own way.

Offering yourself or your resources activates your higher qualities when there is an intention of benefitting others, helping others create happiness, or alleviating their suffering. It activates virtuous qualities—such as kindness, compassion, and altruism—enabling you to experience the joy of expressing the highest version of yourself. The act of giving clearly demonstrates that you have more than enough of something to share with others. In addition, you receive the utmost joy in being able to use your resources for something that aligns with your important values. Because of this, you receive more than enough joy through the act of giving, and you do not need anything in return.

The more you practice the act of giving, whether small or big, the more you'll experience joy, which will amplify abundance in your life.

Gratitude

Years ago, when I experienced my Dark Night of the Soul, one of the messages I received from my heart was: "You're not alone". Then, I thought, *what does that mean?* I kept asking myself this question every day. The answer came to me in a surprising way. It happened when I was walking outside and noticed a beautiful flower on the sidewalk. In that moment, I noticed I was picking up a positive energy from the flower; it was a refreshing, energizing, and hopeful energy. Then, the next moment, I realized that maybe it wasn't that I was picking up the energy, but the flower was sending the positive energy to me to encourage and empower me, to help me overcome my situation. I became so grateful for receiving such nice feelings from the flower. I felt it cared for me.

This thought changed everything. I looked for other things that might be sending me energies. I looked up and found a beautiful, blue sky with gentle sunshine. I felt the sky was delivering peaceful and empowering feelings to my heart, and I became so grateful for what the sky was giving me. Similarly, I started to be grateful for every interaction I had with other people. I felt warmth in my heart when an employee at a coffee shop greeted me with a joyful voice and smiled at me. I felt loved when I received a phone call from my family and close friends. I felt more connected to others when I interacted with them on social networks. I looked for more and found many other things that were helping me—trees, insects, dogs, cats, a gentle breeze, and so on.

Going through a day feeling grateful for the little things in life, I thought, *wow, many things are really helping me experience happiness. I didn't ask for it and they don't get anything in return from me, but they do it anyway! I feel cared for and embraced. I am not alone. I am loved.* The message was right; I am never alone! In fact, I can't be alone! At that moment, there was a surge of gratitude rising inside of me, like an extremely bright light was radiating from my heart. The feeling of gratitude was so powerful that it pushed all the dark emotions away from my mind. I said to myself, "I am not alone. I am one with everyone and everything. I am loved. I am grateful for this opportunity to live this life." This realization enabled me to experience abundance in life and know there was plenty of love surrounding me.

To create abundance in your external world, you first need to experience abundance in your internal world. The first step is to experience gratitude for what you already have at the present moment. Because of our survival instincts, we are wired to search for potential dangers, and therefore, we tend to focus on what is not enough, thereby triggering thoughts and actions based on scarcity beliefs. To experience abundance, you must re-wire yourself to search for what is enough in your daily life. One easy and effective way to do so is to make it a daily practice to search for gratitude in your life. Every night, before you go to sleep, remember what happened throughout the day and count ten things you are grateful for. This helps you create a habit of looking for good things in your life instead of trying to find something that's wrong, and it helps you build stronger faith and trust in your life.

When you practice daily gratitude long enough, it becomes easier to find things to be grateful for throughout the day and stay in a good mood for a longer period of time. Over time, your behavior will start to reflect your feelings of gratitude, and people will notice that. As you keep living your life like this, something magical will start to happen; people will start to show gratitude back to you, and naturally, you will experience more good moods, good relationships, and good opportunities. Yes, good moods and good relationships bring you good opportunities!

Exercise: Daily Gratitude
To turn this into a habit, do this exercise every night for twenty-one nights before going to sleep.

1. Think back to everything that happened throughout the day.

2. Identify ten people or things you are grateful for and imagine sending gratitude to them.

Challenges against Abundance

Fear prevents you from experiencing abundance. Fear takes away your virtuous qualities and activates the worst version of you, triggering negative emotions and bringing out lower qualities, such as selfishness, self-criticism, and powerlessness. Even when you have a lot of material possessions, if you're experiencing lower-vibrational feelings, such as anger or sadness, you are not abundant. You might be able to experience physical satisfaction, but you won't be able to experience true happiness or joy.

So, how can you overcome abundance challenges? By seeing the high qualities in everyone and everything, including yourself. This enables you to experience joy at every moment and attract people and things with the same high-quality energy. If you are going through any of the challenges we discussed in prior chapters, I suggest you prioritize working on them because their negative influences on abundance are substantial. For example, emotional dependency makes you susceptible to others' emotions, thus limiting your ability to co-create. Shame and guilt make you doubt the presence of your good qualities. A competitive mindset pushes others away instead of allowing you to see the good qualities in them.

But there are other challenges, aside from the ones we've already discussed, that can limit your abundance, like a lack mindset, an obsession with wealth, feeling superior or inferior, feelings of sadness and regret, or monetary confusion.

Not Enough for Everyone

The biggest fear that stops abundance is the fear of running out of something, that there is not enough for everyone. This fear makes people behave defensively, selfishly, and competitively.

If you believe there is enough of everything for everyone, your brain searches for information that matches that belief, and you think and act accordingly. You activate inner qualities, such as peace, confidence, and kindness, and you present relaxed facial expressions and a gentle tone of voice that attracts like-minded people. Together, you'll support each other and collaborate, leading to prosperity as a group. There, an inner experience of abundance is manifested into external abundance.

However, the beliefs, perspectives, and pains from the past trap us in an illusion that is the opposite of abundance: scarcity. Scarcity means there is not enough, whether it is food, water, land, or energy. If you believe in scarcity, your brain searches for information that matches that belief, triggering fears and causing you to think and act accordingly. With a scarcity mindset, you'll activate defensiveness, selfishness, and competitiveness. Your facial expressions will show nervousness, the tone of your voice will become tense, and your behavior will demonstrate the energy of scarcity, which will attract like-minded people. Instead of working together, these people will compete against each other for survival, using "survival of the fittest" as the norm.

This fear-driven situation happened in my neighborhood. In the middle of March 2020, I came back to Los Angeles from a business trip and went grocery shopping the next day. There, I encountered a situation I had never seen before; there was no toilet paper, bottled water, or milk. Many food products were sold out. Because of the novel coronavirus outbreak, fear-based thoughts were activated in many people, which led to panic-buying behaviors at grocery stores. On the internet, I saw pictures of people who were driven by these fears with shopping carts full of eggs and toilet paper. How would they consume all those things? Others competed over face masks, and somehow, there was an increase in America's gun sales. Fortunately, the grocery stores were populated with more supplies soon after, which meant they really wasn't a need to buy such large amounts of food, and no one needed to compete with each other. Those fear-driven behaviors caused a situation where stores were temporarily emptied, thereby creating an illusion that there was not enough for everyone.

To prevent this, you need to believe there is enough for everyone. But how? To believe in abundance, you need to know that at least one thing is abundant in your life: your inner resources. Our inner virtuous resources, like kindness, peace, confidence, playfulness, and bravery, are abundantly available. There is no limit to kindness, happiness, peace, or bravery. Now, if there is one thing that runs behind each of these inner resources, one thing that is sourcing all inner resources, what might that be? Behind kindness, compassion, strength, and altruism is love. Love is the source, the origin, the building block of everything within us that manifests into everything outside of us. Love is the one thing that really gives us abundance.

Note that love in this context is not about romantic love, but it is much broader, a capacity to embrace everything and everyone, regardless of the situation or conditions. Some people call it universal love. It is all-inclusive, all-pervasive, unconditional, and unlimited. It is about embracing diversity and accepting that every life and inanimate object is living its own precious life in its own way. You must accept that everything is one organism and give equal importance to it all. Other kinds of love, such as romantic love, a mother's love, and platonic love, are also precious, but they are different expressions of this all-pervasive love; they can only be directed toward individuals, objects, or purposes. Remember the feeling of falling in love? Did you feel the love was as important to you as the entire universe? What about your love for your child? Or your love for those whom you call 'best friends'? These are precious and beautiful, but they are different from the universal, all-inclusive, all-pervasive, unconditional, unlimited love I am referring to.

Love exists in our hearts. Love is the root source of every inner resource, and they are all infinite and abundantly available. By embracing and activating your inner resources, you can empower yourself to take action and make things happen in the external world. This is the reason many spiritual teachers say, "All you need is within you now." You have everything you will ever need at every moment. By choosing to believe in love over fear, you can create an abundant life.

Exercise: Inner Resources

1. Think back to the best moment of your life. An example would be when you were hugged by somebody you loved, achieved something significant, or had a baby.

2. Ask yourself: What virtuous qualities were present? (Examples: Peace, joy, gratitude, confidence, creativity, resourcefulness, sacredness, compassion, safety, etc.)

Obsession with Wealth

Wealth, prosperity, money, and material possessions are physical manifestations of internal qualities, and you can experience abundance through them, but they can cause challenges if they are coming from lower-vibrational intentions and qualities, such as defensiveness, selfishness, and competitiveness. A lot of rich people are unhappy because of this. The typical situation I've observed is an obsession with wealth, prosperity, money, and material possessions. When you're obsessed with acquiring more of these things, "acquiring more" becomes the purpose in itself. When you get trapped in this obsession, it can trigger fear-based motivations, such as—"If I don't acquire more, it will be taken by someone else, and I will become smaller and inferior to them." It pushes you to compare yourself to others and drives you on the quest of "acquiring more," putting you in a competitive mode.

This obsession also invites a fear of losing what you have already. You become afraid of someone taking your money away, which causes anger, frustration, doubts, and distrust in others. Eventually, you find nobody around you whom you can trust, and you experience loneliness and a lack of real connections in your life. Even if you have wealth, prosperity, money, and material possessions, your inner life becomes turbulent, leaving you with no chance to experience real abundance.

When this happens to you, you need to remember that acquiring money and possessions is not the real purpose of life. Money and possessions are simply tools that can give you feelings and experiences that remind you of the virtuous qualities within yourself, such as strength, compassion, and gratitude.

Let's say, you have a luxurious car. An obsession with wealth might have shown you an illusion that this car can make you look fabulous, superior to your friends, and demonstrate your status and significance. But let's drop that thought for a moment and search for the high-quality aspects of that car. Perhaps it gives you a feeling of safety from its security functions, elegance in its color and shape, or gentleness in the way it cruises down the highways. You love all of these virtuous qualities, and the car allows you to experience them.

As another example, let's say you have a successful business that generates good income. Instead of worrying about declining sales or someone taking money from you, it's better to observe what qualities your income activates within you. Perhaps the income gives you a feeling of safety and freedom, and it might also represent the trust your customers and clients have in you. You can even think about ways to utilize this money to give the same experience to others. Perhaps you can use the money to reward your employees' performance, and let them experience the safety, freedom, and trust you've experienced. By doing so, you can use your wealth to spread virtuous qualities to many others. Isn't it a better use of your life to share your wealth and activate good in society instead of worrying about losing it?

Exercise: Virtuous Qualities

1. Consider all the things you love in your life. Perhaps it's family time, a comfortable residence, an exciting business, or a joyful time playing golf.

2. Ask yourself: What virtuous qualities do these things activate in me?

Superior/Inferior

Have you ever had somebody ask you about your occupation, residence, material possessions, or financial assets soon after meeting them? There are people who evaluate others by their financial values, and they change their behavior accordingly. They need to decide whether you are superior or inferior to them based on your finances. If they decide they are superior to you, they will explain to you how valuable they are. If they decide they are inferior, they will either try to devalue you or keep their distance. These are the peo-ple who want to make more money to be superior to others. They want to have more money and experience more luxuries than others, so they can feel superior. When they come across someone who has more, anger and jealousy arise, and they do their best to compete with them. The anger comes from their fear of being inferior to others and becoming small, less valuable, and less worthy. Jealousy comes from the idea that there are limited resources, and somebody is taking the resource away from them.

The quest for superiority will never give us the true feeling of abun-dance because it is a never-ending quest. The quest is motivated by the desire for significance, and the main cause is the way they identify their self-value, self-esteem, or worthiness. Because they identify their values with external things, they do their best to increase their significance by acquiring money and material possessions, but they will never really experience feelings of abundance because there will always be someone who has more.

To experience abundance, they need to stop identifying themselves based on external factors and start identifying themselves internally. They need to understand that no matter what their financial value is, their worthi-ness stays the same, and every living being has equal value.

Exercise: Identifying Worthiness Within

1. Think back to a time when a stranger was kind to you. Perhaps somebody gave you directions in a foreign country, picked up your belongings on the street, or greeted you when you walked into a store.

2. Consider why these people were kind to you. It was not because of your financial values or material possessions, so why?

Sadness and Regret

At the age of eighteen, Maria wanted to study at a university, but she wasn't sure if she could share her desire with her family. Her father worked for the local manufacturing company, making just enough to pay the bills and support the family; he couldn't afford anything beyond the necessities. There were some occasions when her parents argued over money, and it made her insecure and worried. If Maria expressed her desire to go to the university, her father would accept it, but her mother would be stressed about the money. She was scared that she would cause another argument between them. As there was nobody else she could ask for advice, she decided not to pursue university education, and started working instead. She got a job at a local factory.

She enjoyed the job. She was able to establish good friendships with many colleagues, and she worked diligently. In a few years, she received a good amount of recognition, and her income increased enough for her to become independent from her parents and support herself. When she was promoted to be a manager, she started to interact with many more people inside and outside of her company. Eventually, she met Sam. He was gentle, kind, supportive, and had a personality that made her feel at peace and free. They started dating and decided to get married soon after. She decided to quit her job to support her husband's business, dreaming about a happy and peaceful family.

However, the marriage didn't go as well as she had hoped. Sam did not keep the promises they had agreed to as conditions for their marriage, and she learned he was lying to her about several things in his life. She confronted him, they got into an argument, and it reminded her of the arguments her parents used to have during her childhood. It was clear to her that the marriage was a mistake, and she started to consider leaving Sam. However, something unexpected happened; she got pregnant. She wanted to give birth to this new life, and she wanted this baby to have both parents, so she chose to continue the marriage for the new baby.

Fortunately, the baby was born healthy, and it made her and everyone else happy. Maria had to spend a lot of time raising the baby, but it was OK because she loved the baby so much. She felt that the baby was giving important meaning to her life. Sam was also happy about having the baby; however, he didn't take care of the baby at all, using the excuse that he was too busy at work to help. His behavior and lack of interest in the baby was disappointing to her, but Maria chose to focus on caring for her child.

One night, when the baby was one year old, Sam came home drunk, behaving offensively to Maria. As the baby began to cry, Sam yelled at it and hit the baby on its head. Maria shouted, "Stop! Don't do that to the baby!" which made him angrier. Sam hit her across her face. At that moment, Maria felt something break in her heart, and she knew she had to get out of the marriage. She held the baby close, ran outside, and got on a train, not knowing where she was heading. After a while, she ended up back in her parents' house. She didn't want to bother them, but she had no choice. She decided to end the relationship and started living on her own again.

The divorce turned her life upside down and made her miserable. She needed to make money to raise her child, so she tried to go back to her previous job, but they didn't accept her back because of her age. There were high-paying jobs in the market, but they didn't accept her because of her lack of university education. She ended up working three part-time jobs every day and was still only able to make enough to support her living and pay for her child's education. But she had no choice. She had to raise the child that gave precious meaning to her life.

For her, life had never been easy. She felt she had made the wrong decision, and it was too late to turn things around. When somebody said, "You can create your life as you want," she did not believe it. She would say, "It doesn't work that way. Not for me. I've already wasted my life."

I understood why she felt that way, but I still believed she had learned more than enough, and she could create whatever she wanted in her life.

From the perspective of her soul, her life was rich in growth opportunities. When she gave up going to university and started working, she cultivated patience and perseverance. When she got a divorce, she cultivated the ability to stand up for herself, and when she started working three part-time jobs, she cultivated strength, perseverance, and altruism.

Throughout the years of raising her child, she also cultivated the ability to find happiness in the present moment. All of these are precious virtues you can't learn from university education. From the perspective of her soul, her life is precious, special, valuable, and glorious at any level, and I bet her soul is very proud of her. Today, her child is soon-to-be independent, and it is time for her to finally flourish in a worldly sense. With all the virtuous qualities and abilities she has developed, she can create any emotional and spiritual experiences she desires in her life. Yes, our bodies change over the years, and our physical/material manifestations might be influenced by aging, but our emotional and spiritual experiences are unlimited. Maria can create realities that give her whatever emotional and spiritual experiences she wants, whether it is happiness, joy, creativity, contribution, wonder, honor, respect, connection, bliss, or love.

When we are young, we believe in our dreams. We believe that life is full of opportunities, and anything is possible. As we grow up, however, many of us go through challenges and give up our dreams. We still find happiness and joy in different ways, but some may find it hard to accept their life as it is. Comparing their current state to their childhood dreams, they are disappointed with their lives and blame themselves for not being able to do what they wanted to do—provide a good living for their family, or provide a good education for their kids. They regret their past decisions and feel that it's too late to do anything to increase their happiness. Over many years, they build up a deep sadness in their hearts.

Sadness and regret lower your energy, leaving many things in your life inactive. They attract nothing but more experiences of sadness and regret, and these emotions diminish energy flows in your life and largely impact the flow of abundance and money. To heal your heart, you really need to believe in your life. Acknowledge that everything that happened in your life matters, that you have learned enough lessons to turn your life around now, and that you have everything you need to create the life you want now.

Exercise: Healing Sadness and Regret

1. Think back to the moment you first felt sadness and/or regret. Hug yourself as you were then and say, "It's OK. You are safe. I am here for you. I love you."

2. Imagine a beautiful sunshine beyond the clouds of the negative thoughts and emotions in your mind.

3. Say to yourself: I am a survivor. I am strong, magnificent, powerful, and invincible. I am proud of who I am today

4. Ask yourself: If I can create one profound thing by dedicating the rest of my life to it, what would I create?

Confusion about Money

Many people associate abundance with money, but money does not give you abundance by itself, as it is only a resource to create an environment to experience abundance. However, money is essential to many aspects of our lives, and it does affect our experience of abundance. In my client sessions in the last few years, I've learned that money challenges are caused by confusion about what money really is. Therefore, I would like to explain the nature of money, how it can contribute in abundance, and how to attract it.

In its original purpose, money is a sign of gratitude. When you give something to another, you receive gratitude in return. Money is a physical manifestation of gratitude, and you can save and use it for future exchange opportunities. When money is used for the benefit of others out of love, it becomes a physical manifestation of love, and sometimes it can help people more than words can. When somebody is running out of money and doesn't have food to eat, they need money more than words of encouragement. When a child is about to give up going to college due to lack in finances, your money can open the opportunity for them to learn and grow.

Money cannot buy happiness, but money can solve problems in people's lives in its own way. And when your money is used in alignment with your core values, such as supporting the education of underprivileged children, it becomes your agent of good deeds, the force for good. Imagine your money is helping others alleviate their pain, supporting their living, empowering them for success, and increasing happiness in their lives. Doesn't it give your life a more precious meaning? In this way, money can be your agent of love and gratitude. Sure, you can support your living with just enough money to cover your expenses and focus on your life, but you can also experience the joy of making a difference in others' lives if you have financial abundance. When you use your money with love and gratitude, you transfer the beautiful energy to another person, and that energy will spread across many more people—just like a drop of water ripples across an entire lake. Eventually, that same energy will come back to you, giving you more of that abundance in your life.

Because money is essential in supporting our lives today, it can also trigger fear-based energies that stem from our survival instincts. When money is used with these fear-based energies, it spreads that energy to many others and brings the same energy back into your life. This is why many people go through money challenges, regardless of the amount of money they have.

Unfortunately, many people have fears related to money. This is because there are many people throughout history who have used money with bad intentions and have caused fearful consequences for others. For example, authorities have taken money away from people and used it to satisfy their personal desires or gain power in an organization or a country. Or perhaps you might have seen or heard of people fighting over money. These incidents and memories have contaminated the energy of money and have created such beliefs that money is evil and makes people do bad things. Some people take a vow of poverty because of the beliefs that are prevalent in their family line or the community they belong to. However, those unfortunate incidents happened because money was in the wrong hands. Money itself was, and still is, innocent. As discussed earlier, by using money with good intentions, it has the ability to bring love and gratitude to you and everyone else.

Another common money-related fear is the fear of losing it. This fear can cause people to keep their money in a safe place and not utilize it for any purpose. But money is energy that causes an effect by circulating across many people. If you keep it inactive without utilizing it for any purpose, its energy freezes and becomes stagnant. It's like being an overprotective parent who keeps their child indoors all the time. It might be safe, but the child will never be able to express their true potential. To liberate the energy of money, you should invest it in things you believe are valuable and meaningful. That would activate its energy and bring you more abundance.

Another behavior that impedes financial abundance is indifference to money. The people who are indifferent to money simply don't see the importance of money, and they prefer to spend their time and energy on something else. This stops money from flowing into their lives because money is attracted to people who love it and recognize its value. If you love to use your money to experience abundance in your life and share your love and gratitude with others, money will be attracted to you. Sure, you can experience abundance without money, but money can give you the opportunities to experience more abundance.

People often become indifferent to money because they believe money distracts them from spiritual growth and activates their ego, driving them to low-vibrational behaviors. But I say there is another type of relationship you can establish with money; money can be your agent to do good deeds for others, and spread your core values in the society, which ultimately helps you in fulfilling your mission to help others and grow spiritually. If you are indifferent to money, I urge you to imagine what values you can create for the society and what good things you can do for others with your financial abundance.

Exercise: Healing Money

Emotional pain and fears related to money negatively affect your money life. For example, you might have invested money in stock trading and lost a lot of it. You might have harsh negotiations with clients to lower your profits while still needing to pay a large tax, or your hard work may have ended with underpayment. Whether small or big, such money-related pain continues to lower your money energy and attract it to your life. Heal your money energy and turn it into the energy of love and gratitude.

1. Imagine the energy of money as a small child going through emotional pain.

2. Imagine hugging the child, and say, "It's OK. You are safe. I am here for you. I love you. I honor you as an agent of gratitude. Let's spread love in society."

3. Ask yourself: How can I express love and gratitude with my money every day?

Congratulations!

You've gone over the first five challenge themes from emotional independence to abundance, and you've resolved many unfinished businesses from adolescence. You've made progress in your spiritual growth, have allowed yourself to receive abundance, happiness, and joy, and have become ready to proceed in your life missions.

Fulfilling your life missions will give you the utmost joy and the highest spiritual satisfaction. It's a journey to discover your Phoenix, your own divinity through your authenticity. In a sense, your life has been preparing you for this since birth. That is the real treasure you seek in this lifetime.

In the next two chapters, I'll discuss what might happen on this journey and offer some guidance on how to cope with it.

STAGE 6. AUTHENTICITY

As you make progress in overcoming challenges in life and growing as a person, eventually you arrive at a crossroad in life. It is an opportunity for you to go on a path of spiritual development, and it usually starts with a calling.

Calling

A calling can come to you at any age, but I have seen many people receive it in their late 30s to late 40s. It typically comes to you as a thought that questions the learned ideas of your life purpose, values, and identity.

Am I *really* happy?

Is my life today meaningful?

Do I want to spend the rest of my life like this?

Typically, these thoughts come to you when you've established some sort of stability and peace at the expense of your spiritual needs. This is a calling for you to journey into your inner world to discover who you truly are, what you really want, and why you were born. Sometimes, people receive a calling in a hard way. They experience challenges in their lives that give them no option but to go deep inside themselves. Examples would be burnout from work, a failing business, a miserable relationship, or health challenges. Due to the severity of the situation, it forces you to face the issue head-on, making it an effective calling.

When you receive a calling, it means you are ready to take on a journey to make a leap in your spiritual growth and align your life to your life missions that contribute to others' spiritual growth. This is an extremely important transformation for your soul; the timing for this calling was carefully planned by you as a soul. Even if you don't notice it the first time, you will receive the same calling again and again, until you finally take it seriously.

If you do decide to walk the path of spiritual growth, you go through your Hero's Journey, which is a series of trainings and tests that help you grow. Along the way, you'll meet mentors and allies, and you will encounter challenges and opportunities. The objective of your Hero's Journey is to conquer your biggest fears and fully activate your authenticity. This facilitates an extremely important transformation for your soul and will prepare you to take on the missions you promised to complete in this life.

Are You *Really* Happy?

Let me share with you how I received my calling.

In Japan, on July 6, 1986, we were experiencing the beginning of summer. It was a very hot morning, with strong sunshine beaming on my skin. The sound of locusts filled the air in my hometown, Chiba. My father and mother were already back from the big rose garden nearby, and I was studying in my room to prepare for my entrance examination for universities in Tokyo. It was just one of those typical Sundays we had every weekend. Then, suddenly, I heard my father scream. I ran to his room and found him struggling to breathe. I didn't know what to do and immediately called my mother, who was cooking downstairs. When she came in, he was no longer breathing. My grandmother came in, then my sister. We called an ambulance, and they tried their best. Everyone was crying and calling for my father to come back to life, but he didn't. That was the last day of my father's human life.

Nobody expected something like this to happen to him because he didn't have health problems, and he had been working energetically day and night. It was shocking to me too, but I was more troubled by a strange feeling I had when I realized he died on a very special day for me: my birthday. *Why would a father die on his son's eighteenth birthday?* I asked myself this countless times. I was both sad and angry, and I couldn't shake the thought that I was somehow responsible for his death, not physically, but perhaps spiritually. I felt in my heart that I should carry on his dreams and wishes.

And that's exactly what I've done since then. That year, I entered the same university as my father, and I joined the company my father worked for. I worked hard day and night, and climbed the corporate ladder. When I reached my early thirties, I had met all my father's expectations—a good career, distinguished social status, a stable income, a great family, expensive real estate, a nice car, and so on. I was proud of myself, and I was motivated to keep advancing my corporate career and increase the quality of my life as much as I could, to be better than my colleagues or anybody else. I was proud of how well I was doing on that path.

But life gave me an interesting twist. One day, I was watching a comedy show, and the comedian asked the audience, "Are you happy?" Silently, I said to myself, *Yeah, I'm happy.* The comedian continued, "Are you *really* happy?" This question tricked me, and I was troubled by the emphasis on the word "really". What does it mean to be *"really"* happy? How can you tell? To make matters worse, I felt a gap between my brain and my heart; my brain was telling me I was happy, but my heart was telling me otherwise. Where was this gap coming from? I wanted to find out what was going on. I searched for an answer on the internet, spoke to some experts, and joined workshops. It took me a while, but I finally figured it out.

My brain and my heart are two different things, and they can disagree. My brain responds to questions based on knowledge, information, beliefs, and perspectives I've learned from others. In my case, the definition and conditions of happiness were largely influenced by my father's beliefs and perspectives. On the other hand, my heart gives me truthful answers to my questions. My heart does not care about the definitions or conditions of happiness I learned from others; it only cares about the truth of how I feel. So, what does this mean?

I was always listening to my brain for every decision I made and never cared about how I felt in my heart. It was like I had been living my father's life, ignoring the desires in my heart for many years. This was a shocking realization; it was as if my life was false. But I also realized I had precious experiences during this time of being brain-driven. After many days of contemplation, I reached a conclusion. I was grateful for all I had experienced until that day, thanks to my father's teachings, but I promised myself that I'd follow my heart and create a life that would make me *really* happy.

Today's education system teaches us to focus on acquiring knowledge and making logical decisions. Even if you have something you want in your heart, it was easily rejected by others' logical reasons, and inevitably, you dismissed what you had in your heart. Over the years, thinking became the primary dictator of your life, and you lost touch with your heart completely. This is why many people know what they should do or who they should be, but they do not know what they really want. Your heart is the window to your soul that knows why you were born to this life, what you want, and where you are heading. To be the best version of yourself and create the greatest joy, happiness, and fulfillment, you need to follow your heart.

Shifting from your brain to your heart is a major transformation that occurs before you discover your Phoenix. Many people experience a calling to make this shift in their late thirties or early fifties. My calling came through the realization that my conditions for happiness were not mine, but there are many other ways to experience such a calling.

For example, you might experience a lack of meaning in your work and be compelled to find something real. You may ask yourself, "What is the meaning of my work? Who do I want to be as a person? Do I want to spend the rest of my life like this?" Remember, the purpose of your life is not just to survive. It's to grow spiritually and be of service to others. If you focus on survival and spend your days avoiding risks, you might get physical satisfaction, but you won't get spiritual fulfillment. Imagine yourself as a ninety-year-old and look back at your life. What would you be most proud of? What might you regret?

Staying in your comfort zone and avoiding risks might give you an easy and peaceful life physically, but your life is far more than that. You are more than your body. You are a spiritual being that is capable of developing great qualities and being of service to others. Opening your heart and activating your authenticity is the door that takes you to the most joyful and fulfilling life you planned for yourself, a life that burns brightly with the fire of your passion. This is what makes you the hero/heroine of this game of life.

Exercise: Listen to Your Heart

To shift from your brain to your heart, you first need to start feeling what's in your heart and listening to what it tells you. Your heart is the window to your soul and the way to access your authenticity. By listening to your heart, you reconnect with your soul and activate your authenticity.

1. Imagine going inside your heart and feeling the huge space of peace and warmth.

2. Ask yourself:
   Am I *really* happy?
   Is my life today meaningful?
   Do I want to spend the rest of my life like this?

Hero's Journey

This experience of following your heart and going into the unknown creates your very own journey. It is a way to your authenticity. There is no map to follow, nor is there clarity on how to make it happen. You see only what's in front of you, and you can't see too far. Your heart is your compass, giving you directions to let you know whether or not you're on the right path.

In many respects, the path of spiritual development resembles the Hero's Journey as portrayed in *The Hero with a Thousand Faces* by American literature professor Joseph Campbell (1949, Pantheon Books). In the book, he discusses his theory of the journey of the archetypal hero shared by world mythologies.

First, the time for spiritual development comes to the hero as a calling for adventure. Should the hero decide to travel down the path, he/she will undergo a series of lessons and challenges to arrive at a time where they will need to face their deepest fears. Upon conquering those fears, the hero can decide to go back to the original world and share his/her lessons and realizations with others, making a positive difference in the world.

The entire journey in Campbell's model shows as many as seventeen steps, but here is my version summarized in three.

Step 1: Departure

The hero identifies a calling for adventure into the unknown. Fears tempt the hero to refuse the call, but with encouragement and inspiration from a mentor, the hero takes a leap of faith, crossing into a field of adventure.

Step 2: Transformation

The hero goes through a series of trainings and tests, and begins his/her transformation. Along the way, the hero meets mentors, teachers, allies, and enemies. From time to time, the hero also meets various temptations that try to get them off the quest and back to where they came from. The hero is confronted with an ordeal, the ultimate power that tests them against their biggest fear. After a number of attempts and failures, the hero finally conquers the ordeal and wins an elixir as a reward, which the hero can use for the benefit of others. The hero is transformed.

Step 3: Return

The hero decides to go back to the original world and share what he/she has learned. The hero overcomes resistance and helps others transform, making a positive difference in the original world.

Leticia's Story

Let me give you an example of a hero's journey.

Leticia married Robert when she was twenty-seven. He was a wealthy man and promised her a prosperous life, but she didn't know the marriage was going to give her important tough lessons to learn.

Just like many other couples, they tried to get pregnant and have a baby, but they didn't succeed for a while. Instead, something unexpected happened; Leticia suddenly fainted at her parents' house and experienced a lot of bleeding. She ended up going into blood-loss shock and was sent to the emergency room to have major surgery and a couple of blood transfusions to keep her heart pumping. She had an ectopic pregnancy that the fetus could not survive, and she suffered from life-threatening internal bleeding. This was devastating and painful for Leticia, but she survived.

She didn't give up on pregnancy and decided to do in vitro fertilization to increase the chances of success. Three embryos were introduced into her womb, but the test came out negative. They didn't survive. This made Leticia very sad. As the days passed, her period went back to normal, and she said to herself, "Well, next time, we will have a baby."

The next month, her situation became weirder. She suddenly started feeling dizzy and went to see the doctor. Her pregnancy test at the doctor's office came back positive, and she was incredibly excited. However, the doctor couldn't find anything on the ultrasound. Strange. "Let's wait a little bit and see how it grows," the doctor said. They gave her hormones, put her on bed rest for a month, and completed an ultrasound again. Again, there was no sign of a fetus. Something was not right. After extensive investigations through biopsies and other testing, the doctors finally found out what was going on: There was a fetus in her womb, but unfortunately, it was defective and became a cancerous tumor.

The tumor could easily spread to her liver and other organs, so the doctors decided to put Leticia on chemotherapy. She survived, but it had some side effects. She lost her hair and her eyebrows, stripes began showing up on her nails, her tongue burned so bad it was hard to eat or sleep, and she was always tired, nauseous, and depressed.

Her husband made the experience even worse for her because he was absent. He never went to support her during her chemotherapy treatments, and he was never present at her doctor appointments, except for the first meeting when the doctor informed them of a possible pregnancy. Her husband blamed her, saying he would leave her for a healthy woman if she kept suffering. His mother criticized her too. This made Leticia sad and angry, but she managed to distract herself by focusing on everything that was happening in her body. She said to herself, "I have to focus on myself. I have to survive."

One time, her husband came to visit her during a chemotherapy treatment with his shirt turned inside out. She concluded he was cheating on her, but she didn't have energy to do much about it. Still, she confronted him, and said, "Are you trying to find another person to replace me? I am not planning on dying. I am focusing on healing and surviving. When I heal, we will talk about this." Coincidentally, Leticia's father got sick at the same time, which put her entire family under even more stress. She could not lean on her husband, her parents, nor her other family members. The situation pushed her to the edge, and she cried out to God for help.

"God, why is this happening to me? Why me? What did I do wrong? I am afraid of dying. I don't want to die! Why does everything have to be so difficult for me?"

There was no answer.

She decided to deal with everything by herself. She was sad that she couldn't become a mother, and losing her hair was traumatizing, but she focused on surviving and continued to pray to God. The doctors ordered two more rounds of chemo, and her treatment continued for several more months.

One night, she had a dream. God showed up in the dream and told her everything was going to be alright. Some days later, her cancer tests came back negative; she was finally in remission! Even though she fought through the situation alone, she knew God was always with her because He sent her a message that she would be alright.

Over time, her hair started to grow and she regained her strength, but the process was very difficult. She had panic attacks more than thirty times a day, she fainted everywhere she went, and her period came very weak. She continued receiving medical treatment but didn't feel like things were getting better, so she stopped showing up for her treatments at the hospital. She decided to look for healers who practiced alternative medicine to help her with her panic attacks.

This was when she began to meet people who helped her grow spiritually. She met a healing teacher who was able to help her ease the situation. Her health improved little by little, and as she regained her energy, a thought started to arise from within her.

"I have to enjoy life day by day because I never know when I am going to die, and I want to explore new possibilities in myself."

Leticia realized she wanted to do things she never thought she could, and she took it upon herself to explore new opportunities. She had been a dentist prior to her cancer diagnosis, but she decided to go into business administration. She started working in a company as an administrator and went to school at night to learn business management. She started learning meditation and yoga as well, and it made her feel good and helped her immensely with her panic attacks. She tried some healing techniques and experimented with hypnosis too.

Three years after her chemotherapy treatments, Robert was still cheating on Leticia. She was not happy in the relationship; it was clear that the love was long gone, and she no longer felt admiration for him. He even told her he didn't love her anymore and left the house for four months to be with his mistress, but she couldn't leave him. She was so afraid of being alone, so she chose to stay. In hindsight, she said, "Back then, I didn't get my peace because I didn't make myself responsible for my choices."

Leticia's desire to become a mother never faded away, so Leticia and Robert decided to adopt a child. It took them three years to complete all the paperwork and go through the process, but she finally had the opportunity to be a mother, which made her so happy and blessed. Then, they decided to adopt another child. This child involved even more paperwork, but Leticia was so excited and fell in love with this second child. She spent some weeks with the child before the date she would officially receive the baby from the birth mother. But then, at the very last moment, the birth mother changed her mind and refused to sign the adoption agreement. It was shocking to Leticia, and she spiraled into a pit of despair, but she had had an intuitive feeling that it might happen, so she was able to prepare herself beforehand.

Back then, she constantly asked God if she should stay in her marriage or leave. She thought the rejection by the birth mother was an answer from God, so she finally decided to leave Robert and raise her child by herself.

After the divorce, she became incredibly angry at Robert. This anger manifested into a physical illness and caused intense reflux and diarrhea. Doctors said her physical body was clean and that it was more of a psychological issue. She looked for somebody to help her and found a healer, who was able to help her get rid of the diarrhea in just one session. Her healer said, "Leticia, it's your time to start helping others. You came here to serve. You need to start working on that."

This pushed her to begin her new journey to help others. She started meditating every day with a group of healers, to pray for everyone's wellness. She also started helping others in private sessions, and working hard to be a good channel for healing energy. She didn't promote her private sessions in any way, but people came from all over for her help.

After several years, her life changed dramatically. Her child grew up to be a joyful angel in her life, giving her the energy and motivation to live every day. She did very well in business and became the CEO of her company. Her healing activities expanded, and there were several investors who were interested in her work. She proposed that they build a wellness center and they agreed! It was a big surprise for her that made her immensely happy.

The wellness center project enabled her to expand her healing activities even more. She was happier and healthier, but inside, she still suffered from intense anger toward her ex-husband and reflux in her stomach. The anger got even worse when she was informed that her ex-husband was expecting a child with his mistress. She had learned various healing techniques over the years, but they hadn't worked at all on her anger. She worked even harder on her health, incorporating more healthy food, healthy habits, and help from healers, but the anger did not disappear. Still, she refused to give up.

This was when I met her. I didn't know anything about what had happened in her life, and I was puzzled by her situation. From anybody's viewpoint, she was successful, yet she was suffering from anger and various health challenges.

During my healing sessions with her, she was scared and angry at her ex-husband and God. We had two healing sessions and managed to heal a lot of her emotional pain, but our work was not complete. On the last day of my visit to her town, I finished all other work and was ready to fly back home when a thought rose up inside me. "I can't leave until I complete Leticia's healing."

I quickly called her, and we managed to find time for our third healing session that day. During the private session, she sobbed, trembled, and cried out loud. I knew we were onto something. After an hour, we finally completed the healing, and she had let go of her anger and found peace and safety. She was shining like a butterfly breaking out of its cocoon. She was reborn and fully alive, ready for her new life.

After a while, she shared her feelings with me.

"I realized everything was my soul's plan. You know, you cannot expect an orange from an apple tree. I cannot expect my ex-husband to give me the love I wanted because his concept of love was very different from mine. It's just who he is. It was my soul's plan to learn throughout my relationship with him and grow. I needed to learn to forgive. I had many difficult experiences, and it took me a while to forgive and know I am strong enough to heal myself.

"For many years, I felt like life was so unfair. I was angry with God. I almost died, you know. And I had to go through all those challenges by myself, alone. But this realization that it was my soul's plan changed everything. Now I know God was always with me, holding me. Even though I sometimes didn't feel Him and felt alone, He was always there for me. And God guided me to you, Hiro, to be the channel for me to finally heal my deepest emotional wounds and let go of the anger. Now I am at peace with God. And I am at peace with life.

"Today, my focus is on my mission and my loved ones. I thought I always knew why I was helping people, but it has become much clearer and stronger. I have confidence in my mission and my connection to all the power inside me. I direct my energy to my mission and myself for a happy, enjoyable life, and I know that by living like this, I will inspire and empower others, and cause a domino effect that will change the world for the better."

Today, Leticia doesn't feel anger or resentment toward her ex-husband. She feels compassion for him, and she can even laugh at his jokes. They can now co-exist and be good parents for their daughter. She is healthier than ever before—physically, emotionally, mentally, and spiritually. Everything that happened in her life led her to be reborn, like a Phoenix. Now, she is ready for her mission. She is motivated to share her lessons with others and inspire them to transform into their Phoenix.

Notice how she went through her Hero's Journey. She received a calling when she regained her energy after chemotherapy. She met her mentors and allies, and worked on herself to grow stronger and healthier. She arrived at a point where she finally faced her built-up anger and underlying fears head-on. Upon conquering her fears, she received her elixir: a realization that everything was her soul's plan, and that God was always there for her. Finally, she moved on to the last step of sharing what she learned with others to make a positive difference in the world.

This is not a fantasy. Everyone has their own Hero's Journey, and you certainly do, too. As a soul, you planned your own journey and the divine timing to discover your Phoenix. It doesn't have to be as intense as Leticia's path, but your journey is also magnificent and divine. Your Hero's Journey is prepared for you and you alone.

In the following pages, I will share with you some ideas that can help you identify your life missions and discover your Phoenix.

Accepting Greatness

If you are in the middle of your Hero's Journey now, it is imperative to go inside your heart and accept your greatness as a soul. You may need to do some focused meditations to calm down the voices in your mind and connect with the core of the highest and brightest feelings you find in your heart. Here, I would like to share with you a meditation exercise that has helped me and many others.

In this meditation, I ask you to remember your "Fully Alive" moment. This is a moment when you were actively engaged in what was happening at the moment, and had a pure feeling of joy come from within. What might that moment be for you?

Let me share with you my "Fully Alive" moment. When I was fifteen years old, I was in my last year of junior high school. We had about 250 students split into six classes, and I was in the 3-F class. This school liked to encourage competition among its students and classes, and they issued rankings on every possible occasion. My class was the loser, almost always at the bottom rank. In addition to that, I did something to break the school's code of conduct and was sort of grounded for a couple of weeks. The teachers blamed the entire class for my wrongdoing, so the atmosphere of the class was darker than ever. I remember my fellow students looking down, being less energized and less confident in themselves. When it got closer to another competition among the classes, my classmates were already convinced we'd lose again. It was a running competition, and I was selected as the last runner. To be honest, I didn't believe we could win either.

However, as I waited for my turn to run in the competition, I started questioning the situation. "Why can't we win? We are as strong as the other classes. We can win, and we should win!" When I received the baton from the previous runner, we were in seventh place out of eight classes. Everyone in my class had already given up and accepted the loss, but I was so motivated to win the race. I ran as fast as I could, and one by one, I passed many of the other classes. I passed the last runner right in front of the finish line, and we won first place!

What happened after that was phenomenal. My classmates jumped around and came to hug me! Trust me, this doesn't happen much in Japan. Everyone—including students in the other classes—was excited about what happened in front of their eyes. At that moment, I experienced very special feelings; I felt like we were all connected as one being, experiencing this excitement together. Everyone was inspired to believe that anything was possible, and I felt like I had become an inspiration. It gave me a mixture of joy and ecstatic feelings, and my entire being was present. I felt fully alive at that moment.

What is your "Fully Alive" moment? Some of my friends have told me they felt fully alive when they had a baby. They experienced such a sacred, special feeling in that moment. Others have said they felt fully alive when they received recognition from others. Choose your own "Fully Alive" moment and follow the instructions to accept greatness.

Exercise: Fully Alive

1. Remember the moment when you felt fully alive as if it is happening now. Notice how you feel in your heart.

2. Ask yourself: How can I experience this feeling in my life today?

Authenticity

What is authenticity? It's the intentions and qualities you have as a soul. Fulfilling our authenticity is about remembering our God-inherited qualities and intentions. With them, you can act on the life missions you have planned for yourself. Life missions are the work of God, the service you offer to other souls that helps them grow spiritually. Through these missions, you experience joy and fulfillment, which are spiritual pleasures you can create while in a human body.

As a soul, you've inherited all virtuous qualities from God—all of them. When you imagine how Mother Teresa served the poorest of the poor, do you feel her compassion? If you imagine Martin Luther King, Jr. making his "I have a dream" speech, do you feel his bravery or inspiration? You can feel them because you have them inside of you already. This is what those famous masters mean when they say, "All you need is within you now." All the virtuous qualities are already inside you. With them, you can do anything and everything.

I believe we all are on a long journey back to our origin, God's presence. In lifetime after lifetime, we activate our virtuous qualities, embody them, and experience more aspects of the magnificent presence of God. As we proceed with our journey, we remember more and more that we are a part of God, which enables us to increase our faith and become able to exist closer to God's presence.

The beliefs and perspectives we learn through life can cloud our consciousness and hinder us from using the virtuous qualities within. Therefore, to use our virtuous qualities, we must unlearn those false beliefs and perspectives. The opportunity to do so will surface in your life in the form of challenges and emotional pains. All the discussions we've had in previous chapters should help you let go of those beliefs and perspectives, and incorporate ones that serve you better. Once you unlearn enough of those beliefs and perspectives, you need to activate the virtuous qualities you wish for. You need to remember the feeling of the quality, accept that you have it in you, and embody it through experience, which means using it in your everyday life. When you start using your higher virtuous qualities, you will attract more opportunities that require you to use those qualities, and naturally, you will be guided to the life missions you planned for yourself where your virtuous qualities can be best utilized for the benefit of all souls.

Uncertainty, Faith, Going with the Flow

Although everyone's journey is different, there is one thing that is common: uncertainty. When you start feeling how you really want to, it will drive you to make changes in your life. For example, you might want to behave differently at work to increase harmony and trust. You might want to go on an adventurous trip, experience new things overseas, or end a relationship to start a new one. These are all attempts to align your life with what you want in your heart. You know these are all the right things to do; however, it's not necessarily easy for your brain to agree with them, especially when you don't see many tangible outcomes in the beginning. Your brain wants clarity, certainty, and safety supported by logical explanations, but your heart-based decisions cannot provide any of these. There is no concrete plan, and you don't know what might happen next. Even if you're committed to following your heart, the uncertainties can trigger fears. What if this doesn't lead to anything? What if I lose everything? How can I survive? The fear of uncertainty is a tough one. It makes you feel like you don't have control over your fate and that your life is dependent on accidental or random luck, triggering powerlessness and helplessness. You might be tempted to stop everything and go back to your old way of life, to live by your brain instead of your heart. But you have to hang in there.

The antidote to the fear of uncertainty is faith. As discussed earlier in this book, life is not accidental or coincidental. It's all planned by you as a soul. If you are going through uncertainty, it means you are heading toward a place beyond imagination, something unprecedented in your life. You have your own unique and special future prepared for you. Trust in yourself and your future. If you don't trust yourself, who will?

Your life is much more than you may realize, and it's this knowledge that makes you capable of conquering the fear of uncertainty and aligning your life to follow your heart. You have important missions and promises to fulfill. By conquering your fear of uncertainty, you're accepting your greatness and the fact that you are more than your body. You are accepting that you came to this game of life for important missions and to be of service to many other souls. This might sound like the chicken and the egg story; you need to overcome the fear of uncertainty to accept your greatness, but you need to accept greatness to overcome the fear of uncertainty. Yes, indeed. To make this work, you first need to accept your greatness with faith and follow your heart. You must have faith in yourself, your life, and God, and make a leap.

Once you've accepted your greatness as a soul, your path becomes a whole lot easier. You are ready to accept unexpected changes in your life because you know that no matter what happens you'll be guided to your planned destiny. You stop worrying about the future and start fully living in the present moment. You enjoy everything in your life, moment to moment. That's the art of going with the flow.

Exercise: Entire Life

1. Imagine watching your entire life from start to the end, as if you're looking at a timeline of events from left to right.

2. Ask yourself:
    What were the biggest lessons I've learned in my life so far?
    How can this life be even more meaningful?

STAGE 7. PHOENIX

Discover Your Phoenix!

The phoenix is an imaginary bird that burns itself and rises from the ashes to be reborn. The symbolic meaning of the phoenix is the resurrection of your soul, and rebirth. As you conquer your fears and activate your authenticity, you transcend your vibrational frequency and regain access to the greater awareness of your highest intentions and qualities within.

Earlier in this book, I shared with you how I got out of my Dark Night of the Soul. It was an experience of conquering fears and restarting my life anew—just like a phoenix rising from the ashes of its old body—and it ended with this incredibly amazing blissful feeling.

Several days later, I got used to experiencing the blissful feeling every day. Then, a burning desire started arising inside me—a desire to share my experiences with others. I said to myself, "Everyone deserves to experience a life without fear!" It's like something had ignited the fire of my passion inside my heart and pushed me to take action. I posted my experience on social media, encouraging readers to focus on conquering their fears and healing their emotions if they ever found themselves experiencing a Dark Night of the Soul. I received comments from so many people saying they experienced a Dark Night of the Soul, too. This was surprising because I thought nobody knew what the Dark Night of the Soul meant, but it seemed like they got it by the name and didn't need an explanation. Soon after, I started receiving many direct messages on social media from people who were going through their Dark Night of the Soul, asking me for advice. There were so many of them. I experienced so much joy in every moment as I shared my experiences and gave some advice. Every time I saw their faces light up after our one-on-one consultations, I experienced a profound feeling of fulfillment, and I said to myself, "This is how I can be of service to others. My life is meaningful. I am used well by God."

When you follow your heart and acquire your elixir, you are no longer driven by survival needs; you are compelled to be of service to others and are driven by a vision to assist all other lives in growing and prospering. That is the state of the Phoenix. In this state, your body, mind, and spirit are in alignment, and you bring out the best version of you and perform at your best. You encounter opportunities that lead you to meet your promised people, and you experience the utmost joy and fulfillment.

Essence of Your Being

Before discussing your life missions, I would like you to contemplate the essence of your being, your core values. They serve as the basis for your aspirations, motivations, and desires because those things must be behind your life missions. Your core values influence your decisions, affect your thoughts and behaviors, and fuel your passion. Your core values are typically described as a set of virtuous qualities and attributes, such as integrity, honesty, fairness, freedom, safety, harmony, and compassion. All virtuous qualities and attributes are important and precious, but there is a short list of qualities and attributes that are more important for you than others because of your experience in the past. Perhaps you experienced a lack of fairness in your childhood that made you realize the importance of fairness, and you can't help but raise questions of unfairness in your life, like "Why do people treat others differently because of their wealth or social status?" Coming from deep in your heart, these questions can serve as fuel for your burning passion to make a difference in the world.

Your core values reside behind all your identities; core values are the purest part of your identity. If you were to introduce yourself to somebody, how would you describe your identity? Perhaps you'd start with your occupation or your family-related roles, such as husband/wife, mother/father, daughter/son. You might also add social and material things, such as wealth, fame, or achievements? And, of course, you would describe your identity by your name, age, and bodily attributes. In this exercise, I urge you to detach yourself from all these identities and roles, and look at what is left of you. What you find in the essence of your being is something intangible, something that is meaningful beyond the physical realm. Typically, people find their purest intentions, such as "I aspire to experience compassion," "I am here to experience joy," as well as their core values, such as freedom, integrity, transparency, peace, and harmony. Go into the essence of your being and find your purest intentions and core values in this exercise.

Exercise: Essence of Your Being

1. Stand in front of a mirror and think of some different ways to describe your identity. Then, take off the masks of your identity and drop them to the side. Repeat this step until you drop all possible identities you would use for yourself.

2. Now, look at yourself without all these identities. No body, no name, no social status, no family roles, no nothing. What is left of you?

3. Ask yourself: What values are most important to me?

Life Missions

Now, what might your mission be? Unfortunately, there is no simple way to identify your mission. When it's time, it will reveal itself. But let me give you some ideas as to what it might be for you. As I discussed in the Game of Life Theory, the purpose of your life must be something meaningful beyond the physical realm, and my theory is that growing spiritually through activating more virtuous qualities is the purpose of the Game of Life. For every game of life, you set spiritual growth goals for yourself to attain in a lifetime. For example, you might choose to attain a higher level of compassion, address your short temper, and cultivate mindfulness in this lifetime.

Although your path of growth will continue for the rest of your life, if you reached the point in life where it's time to activate your authenticity, it means you've come halfway. You've reached a point where you can start to focus more on other objectives of the Game of Life to grow spiritually by contributing to other people's growth. This, I believe, is the nature of our life's missions.

In my observation, after assisting thousands of people in finding their life missions, there are at least five types of missions.

Mission 1: Teaching

You are meant to share what you've learned through your past challenges with others. That can be an important mission. Because you talk about your real-life stories, your passion translates through your communication, and people feel it intensely. Your promised people will relate to your stories, and they will recognize you as the person they want to learn from. Your audience is the people who are going through challenges similar to the ones you've had in the past; therefore, you are equipped to offer the best possible solution to their problems. Remember how challenging your life was? Your audience is still going through those challenges, and many of them are pushed to the edge. They need your help to realize they can change their life for the better.

Your stories can make them believe they can do the same, and they can be empowered to take action and persevere. You can share your purest intentions and core values with them, which will enable your audience to activate the same intentions/values in their lives. You would be amazed to see how much you can help them change their lives, how much you can experience joy and fulfillment by sharing your lessons, and how much more meaningful your life can be. Of course, it'll go very well because this is the promise you made with them, to be of service for their growth. Before you know it, you'll become a great example and an inspiration for many others.

Teaching is the most straightforward approach to sharing your lessons with others, but the format of teaching can vary. You might go to a school and share your knowledge with students, you might organize a seminar/workshop or make a public speech. You can write your experience in books and blog articles or post your message on social media. Or, you might simply share your experiences and knowledge by talking with your family, friends, and colleagues each daily.

Mission 2: Healing

Helping others overcome their challenges is another important mission you can choose to undertake. To do so, you need to make sure a healing takes place in every challenge. Here, my definition of healing is releasing emotional pain, identifying lessons behind a challenge, and changing beliefs and perspectives. As we have discussed so far, challenges happen in our lives for one reason: growth. Therefore, if we turn our backs and avoid facing the situation, the same challenge will occur in our lives over and over again until we grow. We need to face the situation head on, heal our emotional pain, and change the beliefs and perspectives that no longer serve us. You can help others heal from their challenges by listening to them as a compassionate presence, encouraging them to see the situation as a learning opportunity, and guiding them to identify new beliefs and perspectives that they can incorporate in their lives.

You can offer such services to your family, friends, and colleagues in casual conversations, or you can offer it as part of your existing services as a coach or counselor. I have been doing this for more than ten years, and I feel immense joy when I witness somebody transform; literally, their faces light up! It makes me feel like I'm being used well by God.

Mission 3: Leadership

This is about living by your core values and taking on a leadership role to establish, embrace, protect, or reinstate the values of the community you belong to. Core values are the ones you want to experience as much as possible in life, and if your core values are threatened or abused, you might feel a burning desire to correct the situation, whether it be in your family, community, or country. For example, if nature is one of your core values and you are seeing the disastrous effects of climate change, you might feel a burning desire to take action. You might communicate the critical situation to the community you belong to or take on an initiative to make changes in business practices and lifestyles to make a difference.

For the leadership mission, it is essential to have a vision for change. People come to work with you because they agree with your vision. By uniting with others and joining forces, you can create a big movement for change, and you can make a difference in society. Note that you do not need to be in a leadership position to be a leader. Whenever you talk with someone, you can lead the other person toward a vision. Today, we live in a world where one person's voice can reach the entire world. This is the time anyone can initiate important changes for humanity.

Mission 4: Infrastructure

One of your missions might be to provide an environment for others to learn, grow, and live their missions. Even if you do not directly interact with others, you can contribute to their growth by providing an infrastructure. For example, to help spread meditative practices to create more peace and harmony in society, it helps to organize a conference where like-minded people can get together, discuss important topics, and inspire a broader audience toward a particular vision. Or, you can start a wellness center where people can relax, heal, and learn together for spiritual growth.

Infrastructure missions can support many people in fulfilling their missions. When I started healing as a career, I studied from the founder of a healing technique. She teaches people how to do healing on yourself and on others, and she also certifies teachers to teach the healing technique. She has organized a community of healers and teachers, like-minded people who support each other's growth, so all her students can live their mission to heal and teach others in their country. Her healing technique has spread worldwide, and the community has grown very large today. I feel so lucky, grateful, and honored to have been a part of it for many years. This is an example of an infrastructure mission.

There are people who don't want to do public speaking or one-on-one consultations, but they are good at establishing infrastructures and making them sustainable. There are others who are good at speaking and consulting but are weak in the marketing realm. Over the years, I've learned that everyone has their own strengths, and when we work together, we can fulfill our destiny.

Mission 5: Parenting

Parenting is a very important mission a person can fulfill in life. From birth, parents play a significant role in supporting the growth of a child who can, one day, be of great service to society. In addition, you also have the opportunity to grow through parenting. Even if you don't feel like you've done a good job parenting, you still served the purpose of bringing a child into the world.

Of course, this also includes adoption. Adopting a child is such a beautiful thing to do, to receive a child and raise it as their own, to love a child unconditionally for the rest of their lives. Even if a child did not come into your life biologically, adoption takes place because of the promises between the souls of the parents and the child. Think about it: The soul wanted to live a life with those parents, no matter what it took, even if it meant being born into a different womb. There must be a very strong connection between their souls.

Note about Missions

- You can have multiple missions in your life. For example, I believe my missions include teaching, healing, and infrastructure, possibly leadership in the future, but probably not parenting.

- Your mission evolves. I started on a healing mission, then my infrastructure mission was added, and a few years later, I started my teaching mission. Some years later, I realized my infrastructure mission was over, and an opportunity appeared to expand more on my teaching mission to reach a broader audience.

- Some people might feel you should not make money out of these missions. I disagree. If you spend your savings to do your mission, you cannot continue long term. It is totally OK to make money from the activity, so you can continue your good deeds and fulfill your missions. You can use the profits to satisfy your daily needs, have good experiences in your life, and invest in the activity so you can offer even better services.

- When you're ready, your audience will appear. Even if you feel like you're not qualified or don't have anyone to share your knowledge with, people will find you when you've reached the level of your growth where you are ready to share with others. Just stay authentic and start talking. People will find you and ask for your services, no matter what.

- You do not need to quit your current job or leave your relationship to live your mission. You can continue your life today and align your intentions, behaviors, and actions according to your authenticity and missions. Imagine how you can make a difference in your current job with your renewed intentions and mindset? You might be amazed to find out how your current job can serve your missions! The work you felt was boring or uninspiring can turn into a vehicle to fulfill your highest intentions. It is such a magical feeling to know you are already in the right place to fulfill your mission.

Visioning

In the Hero's Journey, a hero receives a calling, makes a leap of faith, goes through trainings and tests, conquers the ordeal, and acquires the elixir. Then, the hero returns home with heightened intentions, with a vision for the original world to change for the better. Since you started following your heart, you've been guided by the purest intentions and virtuous qualities of your soul. You only needed to keep the faith. Here, I would like to guide you on how to satisfy the desires of your mind and body.

Whatever you focus on, you create. By having a clearer vision, you can increase the chances of making your dreams happen the way you want them to. With this exercise, you can tap into the essence of your being and visualize your missions coming out of the purest intentions of your soul.

Exercise: Visioning

1. Think back to the important values you recognized from the previous exercise.

2. Imagine a desirable world where all your important values are well-established, embraced, and protected.

3. Ask yourself: How can I contribute in creating this desirable world?

Preparing for Death

There is nothing to worry about when it comes to death. It is an exit point to complete this physical lifetime, and you will continue to exist as a consciousness in a world that is different from this one. In a way, death is a graduation from a lifelong education and a liberation from physical limitations.

You need to understand that your physical life is a very unique, precious, and effective learning environment, and there are many things you can do to make a lot of positive differences in your after-life without needing to exert a lot of physical effort, even if you only have a few days or hours left. Here's my recommendation of the top five things to do before death.

1. Drop your beliefs about death.

After you die, you will experience whatever you believe about the after-life because you create whatever you believe. For example, if you believe people go to Heaven or Hell, that's where you'll go. If you believe you will sleep in the cemetery, that's what will happen. That's why it's important for you to drop your beliefs about the after-life, and just choose to believe the best possible things that could happen after death—going to the most beautiful place you can imagine and being welcomed by all your deceased family and friends. Whatever you choose to believe will be what you experience after death.

2. Let go of your anger, resentment, regret, and guilt.

After death, you will transition into a new world, whatever that is. This happens within several days after your death, but if you have a strong attachment to your physical life, you will miss the opportunity to transition. Those attachments are things like intense anger, resentment, regret, and guilt. I suggest you drop these emotions so you can move on after death. To do so, complete the forgiveness exercise in this book for all the people who have ever made you feel anger or resentment. Also, forgive yourself for any guilt, regret, or shame you feel. This forgiveness exercise will make a huge difference in your after-life.

3. Heal your heart.

You might carry pain in your heart from the past, which causes sadness, regret, or even guilt. You can't change what happened, but you can still heal your heart and let go of the pain. I suggest you do the healing exercises in this book that are related to your pain situation. Letting go of pain can allow you to feel a lot happier.

4. Be proud.

No matter what your life looks like, it is special, precious, and important. Wealth, fame, and social status do not matter. You lived this life the best way you could, and you survived this far. Think about how you were able to grow through the mistakes and failures. Think about how you helped others smile. Find reasons to be proud of your life and maintain that feeling as much as possible.

5. Express gratitude.

Now is the time to say thank you to all the people around you. Pick up the phone or write letters to your family, friends, colleagues, and acquaintances. Express your gratitude to them. This will allow you to feel connected to their hearts, which will make both of your hearts warm. What's more important than that?

After you experience physical death, you go back home as a spirit to Heaven, the universe, the after-life, or whatever you call it. You will be greeted by your soul friends, who typically show up in the identity they had when you met them in the human lifetime, such as your parents, loved ones, and other family members. If you try to go back home before your time, they will likely tell you, "Go back! It's not your time yet." However, if it is your time, you will be greeted and you'll have the opportunity to review your entire life. During this time, you can go over the lessons learned, confirm unfinished businesses, and identify new growth opportunities. Then, you might choose to go back to a human life again or take a different approach for your growth.

Now, there are some paths people might take after their death instead of going back home smoothly. There are various reasons they may go sideways, and one reason is if someone has a strong attachment to the life that ended. They might refuse to go home and stay in the earth reality without a body. This is the phenomenon known as a ghost. The attachment can be a strong resentment against another person, or it might be a strong worry for someone who was left alone after their death. In addition, someone may decide to take a different path if they have a strong belief they are supposed to go to a particular place, such as Hell. In such instances, they create an illusion of hell and subsequently live there. The third reason is they simply don't realize they've died and they continue to believe they are still alive. For example, when a large group of people dies at the same time, like in a battle for instance, it is possible that they will not recognize their own death and keep fighting in their consciousness.

These people are the hardest to rescue because they don't have a body and cannot be consulted by others in an ordinary way. But you can still help them energetically so they can become free from their painful emotions or limiting beliefs. If you keep feeling sadness or sorrow for them, it aggravates their situations. Instead, what you can do is send them positive energies and beliefs that can transform their energies and enable them to go back home.

How can you send positive energies and beliefs? Simply focus on positive feelings and beliefs associated with the person, and it will be sent to them. For this purpose, the best thing to focus on would be their virtuous qualities, such as love, gratitude, happiness, compassion, and honor. Love and gratitude will give them a feeling of warmth, peace, and acceptance and help them heal their fears. Compassion will enable them to forgive others and themselves and help them heal anger and resentment. To honor someone is to hold them in the best version of themselves and guide their attention toward their highest qualities.

If you know someone who has passed away but might be trapped, just imagine the person and express love and gratitude for them in your mind. Wish for their pain to be eased and released. Imagine the person demonstrating his/her highest qualities to others and themselves, and thank them for being an honorable person.

EPILOGUE

You've left your physical body and are watching it cease to function. It'll be returned to the Planet Earth to be transformed into another form. Finally, you arrive at the final divine timing; you are completing this lifetime.

Before you know it, there is a gate opening in front of you, radiating beautiful lights. It brings you a feeling of peace and warmth, inviting you to come in. Without doubt, you go through the gate and enter a tunnel of lights. After being entertained by layers of beautiful shining lights in the tunnel, you arrive in a big open field. There is no sound or wind. It is simply peaceful and warm.

From a distance, a group of souls approach you. As you look at them, they are all familiar faces—your family members, close friends, and other loved ones. They all radiate beautiful light in different colors. They smile and welcome you.

"Hey, you! Welcome back! How was it?" a voice asks.

They gather around you and hug you. It's been a while since you last saw them, and it makes you so happy to meet them again. Suddenly, you remember the family members you left in the human life. Are they OK? Can they be happy?

"No worries. They'll be just fine. Everything is planned out for them to fulfill their purposes for the highest and best," another voice says.

Gradually, you return to the awareness of yourself as a soul and look at your entire life from a distance. You remember all the lessons you learned, the joyful things you experienced, and the beautiful moments you shared with others. You also make note of some growth opportunities for your next lifetime.

Another voice says, "Hey, let's catch up and have a lot of fun together!"

You say to yourself, "That's right. I don't need to hurry. I have plenty of time because there is no time and space here. Let's have a lot of fun, then manifest for the next life."

You hold hands with all the others and jump into a shining light together to experience all the beautiful places you can imagine until the next time you choose to go into a human life.

MESSAGE TO THE READER

Who do you look up to? You might think about successful people in our time, such as Oprah Winfrey, Michael Jordan, or Steve Jobs. Or perhaps you think of someone in history, like Gandhi, Mother Teresa, or Martin Luther King, Jr. For me, it's my mother. I know this might sound childish, but I'm serious. I know some great people, and I've met many successful people through business, social activities, and so on, but still, I look up to my mother the most. Why? Because she is the happiest person in the world that I know.

As I write this today, my mother, Keiko, is eighty-two years old. Her husband, my father, died many years ago when he was only fifty years old. Her children, my sister and me, live our lives in different places. She lives alone, but she is far from lonely; she has a lot of friends. She plays table tennis at least three days every week and participates in local table tennis tournaments every month. She goes out dancing every week, and she plays mahjong games with her friends as well. On top of that, she goes to the fitness gym every day. Whenever I call her, she is busy and has somewhere to go. She is the busiest person in our family. She is healthy and maintains a happy mental and emotional state. She does not get distracted by negative feelings. She is stress-free.

Several years ago, I was going through a difficult time in my life, and I lost the motivation and will to live. I felt there was nothing I wanted to do any more. In the past, I had always chased after something—business achievements, a happier relationship, more money, or more material possessions. But there was no motivation or desire left anymore. Nothing. Have you ever woken up in the morning and realized there was nothing you wanted to do? It is a terrible feeling. It makes you feel like you are wasting your life, like you are a failure and don't deserve good things in life. I was there. I had hit rock-bottom.

Then, I became curious about how my mother could stay so happy. My mother was getting older, and she had no ambitions for achievements. She did not seek money; her life was well-established without it. She had not been in a relationship since my father died, and she had been living alone for quite a long time. It seemed to me that she had no particular motivation to achieve or acquire anything, yet she was the happiest person I knew. How could she live like that? What made her so happy when there was no opportunity to improve the quality of her life?

As desperate as I was, I ran to her house to see her. I asked her, "How can you maintain such happy feelings every day?" She seemed puzzled but calmly replied to me. Her answer was something I had never expected. "Hiro, I simply do the same thing every day. That is important for me. I find joy and happiness in every small thing I encounter. My intention is to be who I am."

Those words struck me. It was as if I had been missing the whole point of life. People see values in various aspirations in life, like business success, humanitarian acts, brave service, precious knowledge, a happy family, and so on. All of these are something we aim to achieve. Looking at my mother, I realized there was something precious and authentic in ordinary life that gives us great values: simply being instead of doing. This posed some questions in my mind, such as "What really is the meaning of life?" and "What makes people truly happy?"

In the last several years, one of my passions has been understanding the meaning of life. This book is my attempt to put my many different pieces of knowledge together to describe the big picture of structure, environment, and the rules of human life, the Game of Life.

I hope this book has given you some insights and possibly triggered some important transformations for you, allowing you to create more joy, happiness, and abundance in your life.

Be true to your heart.

Discover your Phoenix.

Be the one to ignite passion in others.

Be the change you wish to see in the world.

With Love and Gratitude,

Hiroyuki "Hiro" Miyazaki

ACKNOWLEDGEMENTS

The world is a better place, thanks to people who are highly developed spiritually and lead others by being great examples. What makes it even better are people who share the gift of their time to mentor future leaders. Thank you to everyone who strives to grow and help others do the same.

I give thanks to my family members—Masumitsu Miyazaki, Keiko Miyazaki, Kaori Miyazaki, and Taichi Miyazaki—for their continued inspiration, understanding, respect, and support.

I give thanks to you, Sayuri Sato Hirata, for your continuous encouragement and support throughout this writing journey. I feel lucky to have met you, and I am excited to experience joy in fulfilling our shared vision and mission together. And I give thanks to the team of Aiki Wellness Center that is led by Sayuri Sato Hirata and Carlos Kasuga Sakai for supporting me to deliver my healing method *'Phoenix Blessing*™' to a broader audience internationally.(https://aiki.com.mx)

I give thanks to Angel Ray for being my best friend and candid advisor for many years. Thank you for being an inspiration to live a life of authenticity through your jewelry products and life journey. (https://www.aquarylis.com)

I give thanks to Rose Mihaly, my former boss in my corporate days, for being the kind of leader I admire and strive to become. Her intelligence, compassion, and joyfulness have kept me inspired to grow as a person and a leader.

I give thanks to Vianna Stibal for being a great inspiration as a spiritual master and a miraculous healer. You've helped me grow so much spiritually and have given me opportunities to connect with so many wonderful people in the world.

I give thanks to Claudia Plattner for sharing deep insights with me when I got lost at a crossroad in my life, and helping me find direction during uncertain times. Your intuitive message has always been encouraging and spot-on.

I give thanks to Elaine Cole for encouraging me to write my book and for assisting me along the way. I also give thanks to Gerald Cole for reviewing my manuscript and giving me direction when needed.

I give thanks to Alexandra P. Brown for friendship, inspiration, candid advice, joyful presence, and support for my activities in United Kingdom.

I give thanks to Natalie Yufereva for enabling me to connect with Russian-speaking audience in their hearts and supporting me in providing abundant communication to Russian community. I give thanks to my friends in Irkutsk - Mikhail Sychugov, Natalia Dracheva, Evgeni Drachev, Alexander Zausaev, Uliana Zausaeva - for enabling me to assimilate into the culture and the natural beauty of Siberia, in addition to hospitality and joyful presence throughout my activities in Russia.

I give thanks to Zaituna Maidenova and Saliya Zaidinova for enabling me to assimilate into the culture and the land of Central Asia. I also thank them for supporting me to deliver deeply spiritual excursions in Egypt. That was truly joyful and fulfilling.

I give thanks to Ann Young for helping me expand my reach to Chinese-speaking audience and to experience joy and happiness of the culture there. You enabled me to feel that I have so many brothers and sisters across Asia.

I give thanks to Tanja Wilcken for friendship, inspiration, candid advice, joyful presence, and support for my healing activities in Germany.

I give thanks to Ayda Velasco for friendship, inspiration, candid advice, joyful presence, and support for my healing activities in Colombia.

I give thanks to Elena Karasenko for friendship, inspiration, candid advice, joyful presence, and support for my healing activities in Ukraine.

I give thanks to Maria Mamaeva for friendship, inspiration, candid advice, joyful presence, and support for my healing activities in Russia.

I give thanks to Nagy Szilvia for friendship, inspiration, candid advice, joyful presence, and support for my healing activities in Hungary.

I give thanks to my friends and organizers who have helped me connect with so many people through workshops/webinars in countries including Australia, Austria, Colombia, Croatia, France, Germany, Germany, Greece, Hungary, India, Japan, Kazakhstan, Latvia, Mexico, Saudi Arabia, Spain, Switzerland, UAE, Ukraine, UK, and USA.

To all the individuals I have had the opportunity to heal or be healed by, I give thanks to you for helping me experience joy and fulfillment, learn lessons, and grow spiritually throughout years.

I give thanks to great masters, including (but not limited to) Jesus Christ, Buddha, Thoth, Kuan Yin, and Virgin Mary, for assisting me in my spiritual journey and in my book writing. Without you, this book would not be possible.

Last but foremost, I give thanks to God, the Creator of All That Is, for letting me be in service through delivering the messages in this book to others. I give thanks for the fact that what was in secret has been brought into the light. It has been an honor to be used well by you.

SEMINARS AND WORKSHOPS

"Phoenix Blessing™" is an energy-healing technique developed by Hiroyuki "Hiro" Miyazaki. The seminars and workshops of Phoenix Blessing™ are designed as therapeutic self-help guides to develop the ability of the mind to heal and to experience joy and fulfillment in life.

Seminars and healing programs facilitated by Hiroyuki Miyazaki and certified Phoenix Blessing™ practitioners:

- Dark Night of the Soul

- Money & Happiness

- Soulmate Relationship

- Self-Empowerment

- Joy and Happiness

- Activating Prosperity

Workshops facilitated by Hiroyuki Miyazaki and certified Phoenix Blessing™ instructors:

- Phoenix Blessing™ Practitioners

- Ascenting to Your Highest Potential

- Relationship & Wellbeing

- Awakening the Prosperity Within

- Business Course for Wellness Entrepreneurs

- Mystical Journey in Egypt (Workshop)

Workshops facilitated by Hiroyuki Miyazaki:

- Phoenix Blessing™ Instructors

- Game of Life Theory

- Law of Attraction

- Life Mission Discovery

- Mystical Journey in Egypt (Tour)

For further information about schedules for Phoenix Blessing™ classes, visit our website at https://www.phoenixblessing.com

ABOUT THE AUTHOR

Hiroyuki "Hiro" Miyazaki has seventeen years of experience in business consulting and project management in the financial industry. After nearly missing the 9/11 terror attack in 2001, he began questioning the meaning of life and explored his inner world, eventually finding his passion in the spiritual and emotional domain and switching careers to become a spiritual healer, teacher, and coach. Focusing on being of service to others, his activity expanded globally, and he has helped many people through private sessions and workshops. His authored course has spread to more than thirty-five countries.

Today, Hiro is a published author and a sought-after inspirational speaker, healing teacher, coach, and consultant. He is the creator of Phoenix Blessing™, the emotional healing technique that was invented to heal the toughest emotional challenges brought forth by the Dark Night of the Soul. He was certified as an SIY Teacher, a Spiritual Intelligence (SQ21) coach, a ThetaHealing® Science Instructor/Practitioner, a QHHT practitioner, and a Reiki master.

Hiro was born and raised in Japan. He currently lives in Los Angeles and offers private sessions and self-development workshops internationally. He loves traveling, connecting with people in various cultures, and exploring wonders of the world. He has a passion for learning and sharing spiritual practices from ancient Egypt.

Information about his public workshops, online seminars, and private healing sessions can be found at https://phoenixblessing.com.

SIY (Search Inside Yourself) is a mindfulness-based emotional intelligence training program developed at Google. (https://siyli.org)

SQ21™ is a Spiritual Intelligence Assessment program created by Cindy Wigglesworth of Deep Change, Inc. (https://www.deepchange.com). Spiritual Intelligence is defined as "the ability to act with wisdom and compassion while maintaining inner and outer peace (equanimity), regardless of the circumstances."

The ThetaHealing® technique is a meditation technique created by Vianna Stibal in 1995, that utilizes a spiritual philosophy with the purpose of improvement in mind, body, and spirit while getting closer to the Creator of All That Is. ThetaHealing® and ThetaHealer® are registered trademarks of THInK (https://www.thetahealing.com).

QHHT (Quantum Healing Hypnosis Technique) is a hypnosis technique developed by Dolores Cannon. (https://www.qhhtofficial.com)